Our Future is Free

By Matt Greer

Print Edition

Contents

INTRODUCTION

We know that very different social systems produce very different versions of human nature. The underlying social system we use today is the Monetary System. Money determines how we allocate power and authority, how we make decisions, how we utilise technology, how we interact with one another, and how we interact with the Earth and its resources. It influences almost everything we care about - friendships, government, climate change, education, terrorism, work, housing, war, and health to name just a few. This book examines the far-reaching consequences of a society organised by money and the profound effect it has on the human experience. We see that, ultimately, money proliferates a civilisation that is unintentionally harmful to itself. We also see that a transition away from money isn't a pipe-dream, rather, it's a necessity. An increasingly urgent one too.

Recent studies of more than 130 countries repeatedly show the same thing: Almost 90% of us don't enjoy our jobs. Despite this, we spend the majority of our adult lives doing them. Is all this work necessary to create a world we want to live in though? The short answer is no. The majority of today's jobs contribute nothing toward producing the resources we need to survive and prosper. The majority of today's jobs are fictitious manifestations of a society based on some pieces of imaginary paper (money). Today we use money to buy nice things so we naturally assume it enables a good life. It doesn't though. Money is a shackle, enslaving us into a hypnotic state of social paralysis. It's both destroying the planet and psychologically damaging us.

While the book raises awareness of money's inappropriateness at a fundamental level, it also demonstrates we can do much better. It details our ability today to produce an abundance of resources for all people in a largely automated manner by changing to a moneyless social system. In making such a change we'd gain the time and freedom to express our individuality and creativity, leading to a happier, more civilised, and more sustainable future.

Past failures will be examined, a new approach will be explored, a path to get there will be suggested, and projections will be made about the future implications of such a system. This book is a holistic all-encompassing story about us - where we came from, who we are today, who we could be tomorrow, and how we might get there. To bring the story to life, case studies, research, thought experiments, analogies, and quotes will be utilised.

The book aims to seduce the reader, getting them interested in things they didn't know they were interested in. In trying to achieve this the writing is deliberately provocative and strident, although still maintains its scientific integrity (the book is grounded in current accepted scientific understanding with over 500 references to papers, data, or literature).

Quote
Edwin Hubble – Astronomer
"Equipped with his five senses, man explores the universe around him and calls the adventure science"

While the book is grounded in science, no single study can prove that money is the root of almost all our problems and the barrier to a better future. Money is too intricately weaved into our society and consciousness for one simple experiment to provide such proof. However, with introspection and philosophical arguments underpinned by evidence across a broad range of scientific disciplines, the goal is to persuade the reader of this reality. The goal is to persuade the reader that money is indeed the basis of almost all our problems, and without it, we stand on the threshold of a future almost beyond imagination.

What qualifies the author to write this book? Am I a specialised expert? No, but that isn't necessary because moneys influence on humanity and the wider biosphere cannot be addressed by any one specialisation. It touches on history, biology, neuroscience, sociology, economics, psychology and many more. Rather than being a specialised expert, what's needed is the motivation to understand the core principles of many disciplines and the time to understand the implications of it all. The book doesn't reveal any new discoveries at the coalface of any specific line of inquiry so it doesn't require specialised knowledge. Instead, it takes blue chip information (widely known and accepted) from a range of disciplines and knits this together to tell a compelling story. Most specialised experts don't have the time or freedom to explore this kind of broad multidisciplinary research.

While the book doesn't reveal any new primary research, it does reveal a big picture story that will surprise and excite many. We are moving toward a post-scarcity world. Each year the winds of social change gust a little stronger across the increasingly barren plains of capitalist idealism.

1. DEFINING OURSELVES – WHAT MAKES US HUMAN?

1.1. What are our basic needs?

Our basic needs fall into two broad categories (Physical needs and emotional needs) We're all pretty familiar with our needs for physical well-being:

- Food
- Water
- Shelter (+ clothing)

Beyond food, water, and shelter, what else do we need for our emotional well-being? While some aspects of this still aren't unanimously defined, studies repeatedly show we need[1,2,3,4]:

- Safety & security – having the confidence to stretch ourselves
- Love & belonging – feeling equal, as though we're in it together

These things are essential for our emotional well-being. While food, water, and shelter ensure our heart keeps beating, what good is that if we're not happy?

Beyond our physical and emotional well-being, what motivates us? How are we challenged and fulfilled? What makes us get up out of bed in the morning? And what makes us hit the snooze?

1.2. What motivates us?

Our intuition often suggests that money motivates us. More money doesn't make us happier at work or better at what we do though. In fact,

1 http://www.apa.org/pubs/journals/releases/psp-101-2-354.pdf
2 http://www.theatlantic.com/health/archive/2011/08/maslow-20-a-new-and-improved-recipe-for-happiness/243486/#.TkvKIRv8USE.facebook
3 http://www.forbes.com/sites/christinecomaford/2013/03/13/the-3-things-all-humans-crave-and-how-to-motivate-anyone-anytime-anywhere/
4 http://www.hup.harvard.edu/catalog.php?isbn=9780674059825

— many studies show the opposite to be true[5,6,7,8,9,10,11,12]. So what *actually* motivates us?[13]

- Autonomy - we want to choose what we do, based on our own interests
- Purpose – we want to do something that matters
- Mastery – once we've chosen what matters to us, we want to get better at it

If we're doing things that motivate us we'll have more stimulating and fulfilling lives.

1.3. How does our brain work?

Quote

David Eagleman - Neuroscientist

"Are we free to choose how we act? While it's not yet known whether we have free will or not, what is very clear is that the unconscious mind is the one that's in charge and the conscious bit on top is not the one driving the boat. Most of what you feel and how you act and the ways you behave and the things you believe are all being generated by systems under the hood that you have no access to and no real acquaintance with"

The human brain is the most complex object in the known universe - if we could produce a detailed map of every neuron and connection in just one human brain, that map would contain more data than all digital data created in human history[14]. The average human brain makes roughly 10,000,000,000,000,000 calculations per second[15]. It is a monumental

5 http://blogs.hbr.org/2013/04/does-money-really-affect-motiv/

6 The relationship between pay and job satisfaction: A meta-analysis of the literature; Judge TA, Piccolo RF, Podsakoff NP; Journal of Vocational Behaviour 77 (2010) 157-167.

7 Deci, E. L., & Ryan, R. M. (2000). The "what" and "why" of goal pursuits: Human needs and the self-determination of behavior. Psychological Inquiry, 11, 227–268.

8 Pfeffer, J. (1998). The human equation: Building profits by putting people first. Boston: Harvard Business School.

9 http://www.timothy-judge.com/Judge,%20Piccolo,%20Podsakoff,%20et%20al.%20(JVB%202010).pdf

10 http://www.gallup.com/poll/150383/majority-american-workers-not-engaged-jobs.aspx

11http://www.rug.nl/gmw/psychology/research/onderzoek_summerschool/firststep/content/papers/4.4.pdf

12 http://intl-rop.sagepub.com/content/early/2011/10/19/0734371X11421495

13 Drive: The surprising truth about what motivates us; Pink DH; (2011)

14 https://www.youtube.com/watch?v=A-3z4bEP5OA

15 https://curiosity.com/video/your-brain-is-amazing-piled-higher-and-deeper-phd-comics/?ref=hmv

triumph of the machinery of biology and nature.

All this complexity but *what is it* though? Essentially, it's an information processor. Much like an information processor, our brain is a responding mechanism, it responds to environmental stimuli. Everything we experience physiologically from our environment through touch, taste, sight, smell, and sound is sent to our brain via electrical signals[16,17].

All these experiences from the moment of our conception shape the micro-structure of our brain. Every detail of every experience permeates the subconscious jungle inside our heads[18]. Our subconscious mind then influences the way we perceive reality[19,20,21]. This includes our wants, thoughts, feelings, opinions, values, choices, and behaviour[22,23,24].

Nobody picks their parents, nobody picks the society they're born into, nobody picks the life experiences that shape the development of their nervous system and the connections in their brain, nobody picks the ideas they're exposed to or the impact they have on them. Yes, we may be able to think and do as we want to some extent but where did those wants come from? If our wants are the product of prior causes which we did not choose, do we really choose our wants? There is an unending regress of causality that always ends in darkness. We're at the whims of the ambient culture and genetics that created us.[25]

Research
This study is conducted at Christmas time. Young children are taken to visit Santa in groups of two. Half of them are asked "what do you want for Christmas?", the other half are told "Christmas is a time of giving". Later in a completely different situation, the kids are offered chocolates. There's two chocolates for each group. One chocolate is huge, the other is

16 Soon, Chun Siong; Brass, Marcel; Heinze, Hans-Jochen; Haynes, John-Dylan (2008). "Unconscious determinants of free decisions in the human brain". Nature Neuroscience 11 (5): 543
17 http://us.macmillan.com/thinkingfastandslow/danielkahneman
18 http://www.pnas.org/content/103/19/7524.full
19http://www.goallab.nl/publications/documents/Aarts,%20Custers,%20Marien%20(2008)%20%20preparing%20and%20motivating%20behavior%20outside%20awareness.pdf
20 http://science.sciencemag.org/content/329/5987/47
21 https://www.ncbi.nlm.nih.gov/pubmed/17431137
22 http://www.socialsciencespace.com/2013/01/daniel-kahneman-on-bias/
23 What is psychodynamics? - WebMD, Stedman's Medical Dictionary 28th Edition
24 Corsini and Wedding 2008; Corsini, R. J., & Wedding, D. (2008) Current Psychotherapies, 8th Edition. Belmont, CA.: Thomson Brooks/Cole. (pp. 15-17
25 https://www.youtube.com/watch?v=8JSRXnkVpXo

small. One child is randomly chosen to select a chocolate. In the group who were asked "what do you want for Christmas?", most children chose the large chocolate, sometimes even snatching it away. In the second group who were told "Christmas is a time of giving", most children took the small chocolate and left the bigger one to the other child.

In that study, the fundamental nature of their behaviour was transformed on the basis of a single re-framed statement hours earlier. In the world we're born into today we face countless inbuilt situations that affect us far more profoundly than the framing of Christmas. The bombardment from our culture is so holistic that it defines our nature. Imagine the scope of possible change in our behaviour as a result of meaningful changes to our social environment. The possibilities are boundless.

The way our brain works is essentially the way we work. The fascinating truth is that our brain doesn't really work at all. Rather, it responds, or more specifically, it responds to the experiences from the world around it. Thinking isn't so much something we do as it is something that happens to us[26,27,28,29,30]. Our brains are built on the fly in response to our life experiences. Those experiences impact every fibre of our being and shape the nature of our behaviour.

1.4. What is human nature?

Quote
Michael Tomasello – Developmental Psychologist
"If you raised a child on a desert island with no social contact, their intelligence as adults would be very similar to that of apes. We've evolved to learn from others, communicate with others, and collaborate with others. If there was no-one else there, no culture, no tools, and no language, then that natural human intelligence just wouldn't develop"

---

26 Holton, Richard (2009). "Response to 'Free Will as Advanced Action Control for Human Social Life and Culture' by Roy F. Baumeister, A. William Crescioni and Jessica L. Alquist". Neuroethics 4 (1): 13–6
27 http://selfpace.uconn.edu/class/ccs/Libet1985UcsCerebralInitiative.pdf
28 Smith, Kerri (2011). "Neuroscience vs philosophy: Taking aim at free will".Nature 477 (7362): 23–5
29 http://www.amazon.com/Power-Your-Subconscious-Mind/dp/160459201X%3FSubscriptionId%3D0G81C5DAZ03ZR9WH9X82%26tag%3Dzemanta-20%26linkCode%3Dxm2%26camp%3D2025%26creative%3D165953%26creativeASIN%3D160459201X
30 Eagleman, D.M., Person, C., Montague, P.R. (1998). The computational role of dopamine delivery. Journal of Cognitive Neuroscience. 10(5): 623-630

Is it human nature to do the following things, all of which are common today?

- Learn between 9am and 3pm at school while growing up
- Work five days a week from 9am to 5pm
- Compete with others for wealth, prosperity, and material goods
- Take holidays to escape from our reality

We do these things because we're born into a society that expects us to do these things[31,32]. We observe these things happening and we copy. Remember, our brain is an information processor, it has no mechanism to determine subjective relevance.

At birth our brains are only 25% of their mature weight, less than many other species. Many other species are more hard-wired than we are. Dolphins are born swimming. Zebras can run at 45 minutes old. Giraffes stand within hours. A colt trots shortly after birth. A kitten leaves its mother to forage after only a few weeks. We humans take almost a year to walk though. We're biologically designed to adapt to any environment rather than being typecast to just one. We're biologically designed to let our life experiences shape our nature. Are we givers or takers? Selfish or altruistic? Compassionate or heartless? While some fundamentals are hard-wired (like the ability to read facial expressions), the rest is formed as a response to our social world.[33]

While we feel individually responsible for the development of our own intelligence, this couldn't be further from the truth. We're a collective species. Our level of intelligence today depends on those we've learnt from while growing up.

So what is human nature? It isn't really any one thing. Our natural behaviour is an extrapolation of the culture we're born into and the way we see others behaving in that cultural setting. It's human nature to learn from our surroundings and culture.

Quote
Yuval Noah Harari – Historian
"The heated debate about our natural way of life misses the point. Ever

---

31 http://www.bbc.com/culture/story/20151012-feral-the-children-raised-by-wolves
32 https://www.youtube.com/watch?v=93HymGXC_wM
33 https://www.youtube.com/watch?v=hvTQmE4mmX4

since the cognitive revolution 70,000 years ago, there hasn't been a single natural way of life for us. (There are only cultural choices,) from among a bewildering palette of possibilities"

1.5. What is culture?

Culture is that complex whole representing the capabilities and habits we inherit from society - from the use of technology, to the understanding of language, to the nature of beliefs, to the structure of governments, to social etiquettes, to rules and laws.

We've been evolving for millions of years but for the majority of that time our culture didn't change much. It wasn't until 12,000 years ago we started to abandon the nomadic lifestyle and adopt the settled agricultural lifestyle. This was the most significant cultural shift in human history. This shift in lifestyle shaped the culture we experience today. Just in the last few generations we've been going through another monumental shift, one we're still in the midst of today. This latest shift, enabled by technology, is creating new opportunities and threats at a rate never before seen in human history.

While our culture continues to evolve, it doesn't always get better. Much like biological evolution – which doesn't always result in improvements in the big picture – cultural evolution doesn't always improve our way of life. For example, the advent of consumerism that's metastasized throughout the world over the past few decades has not improved happiness. In fact, it's making many people miserable[34].

It's hard to pinpoint why some things stick in our culture and others don't. For the most part, accidents of historical circumstance are picked up and pressed into service by groups that develop vested interests in them. They use social, political, religious, and economic protocols to perpetuate their cultural beliefs[35].

Our culture has largely been shaped by the complex unintended consequences of human action, but not human design. A kaleidoscopic procession of events, occurrences, and ideas have created the world we know - a journey that's been both chaotic and beautiful.

34 https://www.amazon.com/Sapiens-Humankind-Yuval-Noah-Harari/dp/0062316095
35 https://www.amazon.com/Sapiens-Humankind-Yuval-Noah-Harari/dp/0062316095

Thought experiment

Imagine you're born into a society very different from today. In this society nobody wears clothes and psychedelic drug use is encouraged. Both of these ideas are taboo and almost unilaterally illegal today. Are they really so wrong though? After all, there's almost no more fundamental right – as a living conscious being – than to exist in the form we were born (without clothes). Every other living being on the planet does. A similarly fundamental right - as a living conscious being - is the right to explore different realms of our own consciousness. This is essentially what a psychedelic drug enables. Additionally, there's now increasing scientific evidence that both of these things can be beneficial for our physical and mental health[36],[37],[38],[39],[40],[41].

So, imagine again you're born into a world where nobody wears clothes and psychedelic drug use is commonplace. If you were born into this world, and knew no other, wouldn't it seem rational, logical, and normal that people behave like this? Furthermore, if someone suggested you'd have to cover up and couldn't explore your own consciousness – that these things were to become illegal – wouldn't you be outraged?

This thought experiment isn't designed to promote nudity or drug use specifically. Sorry if this disappoints some of you. Those examples are merely intended to provoke thought though. The realisation here is that our culture seems normal because it's all we know, not because it's necessarily normal per se.

For most of human history we thought our social world was intelligently designed when it fact it was accidentally evolving. Ironically, today we have a culture that can actually enable the intelligent design of our social world, yet our political institutions seem to be accidentally evolving, from left, to right, to left, term by term, adding little of value, perhaps more than ever. The great news is we have social conditions today ripe to

---

36 http://www.sciencedirect.com/science/article/pii/S0163725803001657
37 Casler, Lawrence. "Some Sociopsychological Observations in a Nudist Camp: A Preliminary Study." Journal of Social Psychology 64 (1964): 307-323
38 https://www.ncbi.nlm.nih.gov/pubmed/20819978
39 http://journals.plos.org/plosone/article?id=10.1371/journal.pone.0063972
40 Story, Marilyn D. "Factors Associated with More Positive Body Self-Concepts in Preschool Children." Journal of Social Psychology 108.1 (1979): 49-56
41 http://rspb.royalsocietypublishing.org/content/270/Suppl_1/S117

change this. We can intelligently design a social world unrecognisable from the one we live in today (as we'll see in the coming chapters).

1.6. What are genes?

Quote
Robert Sapolsky – Neuroendocrinologist
"One of the most widespread and dangerous notions today is 'oh that behaviour is genetic'. What does that mean? For most people what it winds up meaning is a deterministic view of life: genes are things that can't be changed, things that are inevitable, things you shouldn't waste resources trying to fix. That is sheer nonsense"

Genes are part of the make-up of our body that affects who we are[42,43,44,45,46]. What do we know about genes?

- At an embryonic stage our genes are passed down from our parents[47]
- From then onward our genes begin changing[48]
- They adapt to best enable us to survive[49]
- They're malleable and change over time in response to environmental stimuli[50]

While it's possible for us to be genetically pre-disposed to certain things, if the environment doesn't support it, the genetic predisposition often doesn't manifest[51,52]. That's because genes can change or be eradicated by the influence of the environment[53]. It is in our nature to change due to nurture.

42 Dusheck, Jennie, The Interpretation of Genes. Natural History, October 2002.
43 Carlson, N.R. et al.. (2005) Psychology: the science of behaviour (3rd Canadian ed) Pearson Ed. ISBN 0-205-45769-X
44 Ridley, M. (2003) Nature via Nurture: Genes, Experience, & What Makes Us Human. Harper Collins.
45 Westen, D. (2002) Psychology: Brain, Behavior & Culture. Wiley & Sons. ISBN 0-471-38754-1
46 http://www.oxforddictionaries.com/definition/english/gene
47 http://history.nih.gov/exhibits/genetics/sect1a.htm
48 http://ghr.nlm.nih.gov/handbook/mutationsanddisorders/genemutation
49 http://www.sciencedaily.com/releases/2008/06/080624174849.htm
50 http://jama.jamanetwork.com/article.aspx?articleid=182138
51 http://www.biologicalpsychiatryjournal.com/article/S0006-3223(05)00775-4/abstract
52 http://www.nature.com/npp/journal/v32/n11/full/1301359a.html
53 Epigenetic regulation of gene expression: how the genome integrates intrinsic and environmental signals; Rudolf Jaenisch1 & Adrian Bird2; Nature Genetics 33, 245 - 254 (2003) doi:10.1038/ng1089

Research
Both males and females are shown raw photographs that naturally provoke emotional responses. Electrodes measure facial expressions to gauge the emotional response. In the instant after seeing the photo (before they become consciously aware of it), males have similar responses to females. However, within a fraction of a second, the male brain freezes the facial muscles to suppress any signs of emotion. This is a learned cultural response. The stereotypical emotionless male, long thought to be an inherent trait of the Y chromosome, is actually a product of our culture.

Case study
In some Asian and Pacific cultures, the third boy in a family is raised as a girl. While there are many genetic pre-dispositions associated with being male, if not supported by the environment they tend not to manifest. Typical male behaviours are taught out of the boy and he behaves in line with typical female stereotypes. This demonstrates the momentous influence the environment of our upbringing has on who we become as adults.[54]

To be clear, this chapter is not trying to suggest it is nurture rather than nature. Of course, it is both. In many situations, genes are strong indicators of future behaviour. Genes have a massive part to play but genes themselves are subject to the influence of the environment. Nothing, including our genes, can be understood separate to the environment.

1.7. Nothing in the universe is self-activating

Quote
John Muir – Conservationist, Author, Naturalist
"When we try to pick out anything by itself, we find it hitched to everything else in the Universe"

Science is yet to find anything that self-activates. Every single atom, cell, or organism requires another atom, cell, or organism to activate it. All

---

54 Bartlett, N. H.; Vasey, P. L. (2006). "A Retrospective Study of Childhood Gender-Atypical Behavior in Samoan Fa'afafine". Archives of Sexual Behavior 35 (6): 659

matter is symbiotic[55]. In other words: nothing just starts doing stuff by itself, ever.

This has important implications for the way we understand human behaviour. While some of us may be pre-disposed to forms of violence, crime, or greed, these aren't necessarily permanent genetic deficiencies. They aren't necessarily permanent features of human nature. Rather, they're activated by something in the environment (our culture). Yes, in some cases they come from our parents, but where did our parents get them from? And where did their parents get them from? And where did their parent's parents get them from? If nothing in the universe is self-activating then no unwanted behaviours are self-activating, nor are they necessarily here to stay. They're only here as long as we foster a culture in which they remain relevant.

That being said, while it may be theoretically possible to eradicate unwanted behaviours completely, it wouldn't be practical to attempt that today, or even in our lifetime for that matter. However, we could seek to improve the way most people behave most of the time if we can design a thoughtfully constructed cultural environment.

---

55 http://www.edquest.ca/pdf/sia71-1notes.pdf

systems ⟵ rules.
social protocols.

2. DEFINING OUR SOCIETY – HOW DOES IT WORK?

2.1. How does society work?

How have we organised society today? What makes it function the way it does?

What we're looking for is a system of social organisation, a set of rules which serve to organise society, a *social system*. It's something that determines legal, political, economic, and social protocols[56].

While there are many layers of social systems, some are more prominent than others. What core underlying social system do we use in society today? What system sets the basic rules globally, in turn defining our society, and in turn defining us?

- Is it government? While we all have governments, some are Democratic, Socialist, Communist, Dictatorships and so on. No government defines our world and everything else in it.
- Is it religion? This system also has many branches, such as Christian, Islam, and Buddhism. Even though 84% of us classify ourselves as religious, no religion defines our world and everything else in it[57].
- Is it corporations? Corporations are also a worldwide institution but each one has different rules and values. No corporation defines our world and everything else in it.

While these institutions play a dominant role in our lives, they don't organise all of society. The one system globally that defines our world and rules above all else within it is *money*. Money is the one thing we all require - no person, government, religion, or corporation can survive without money.

Money has been central to the functioning of human society since the first cities sprung up on the fertile riverbanks of Mesopotamia. It determines whether nations rise or fall, whether democracy functions properly, and whether most people have a job, house, or basic needs

---

56 http://www.theemergenceproject.org/#!glossary/c1xne
57 http://www.pewforum.org/2012/12/18/global-religious-landscape-exec/

catered for[58].

Despite this, most of us know very little about money. We know it arrives in our pay checks and enables us to buy things (or pay off debts) but other than that, few of us know much about money as a system of social organisation. We don't know how and why it was created or how it shapes the world we live in, and consequently, how it shapes the human experience.

Money – or the Monetary System – is the dominant social system defining society. In this chapter we'll explore some of the consequences of a society organised by money.

2.2. How did money come to be?

From our early hunter-gatherer days, we understood the value of co-operating and organising ourselves. Being organised increased our chances of survival. It enabled us to hunt and acquire resources more effectively[59].

What do we mean by *resources*? Anything we can use for our survival and fulfilment, including food, water, energy, tools, shelter, materials, transport, entertainment, and all of the processes, know-how, and technology that goes into producing it.

After recognising the value of co-operation for hunting and gathering, we co-operated to develop more complicated social systems:

1. Developing specialisations and a pecking order within society (Hierarchical System)[60]
2. Which led to a sense of ownership and the concept of gifting (Gift System)[61]
3. As we became more aware of our needs we began to trade (Barter System)[62]

58 http://model-economy.wikispaces.com/
59 John Bintliff 2012 The Complete Archaeology of Greece: From Hunter-Gatherers to the 20th Century A.D. John Wiley & Sons, 19 mars 2012
60 Fagan, B: People of the Earth, pages 169-181. Scott, Foresman, 1989
61 Keesing, Roger; Strathern, Andrew (1988). Cultural Anthropology. A Contemporary Perspective. Forth Worth: Harcourt Brace and Company. p. 165
62 Polanyi, Karl (1957). Polanyi, Karl et al., ed. Trade and Market in Early Empires. Glencoe, Illinois: The Free Press. p. 14

4.   And eventually with so much trade happening, money provided a
     more effective way to measure the value of the things we traded
     (Monetary System)[63]

Money was created when we realised Barter was inefficient. With Barter
it was hard to find someone who had what you wanted but also wanted
something you had. As such, we needed a portable store of value.
Something efficient and convenient. Something to facilitate the equitable
sharing of goods and services between one another[64]. This was the
original purpose of money.

Money is the result of an intelligent species becoming more civilised and
co-operative. It's the most recent and most imaginative social system in
our cultural evolution to date. All our social systems have been designed
to address one common problem: *A scarcity of resources.*

A scarcity of resources basically means there isn't enough stuff for
everyone. All our social systems have been designed to manage our
scarce resources. The key question that laid the foundation for all our
social systems was: *How do we allocate the scarce resources among the
people?* In other words: Who gets what? And why? Money is the latest
tool invented by humans to answer that question.

Over the centuries the core characteristics of money have remained but
the finer details have evolved. At the end of the 19th century, capitalism
became the prominent economic system and – despite a challenge from
centrally planned economies (like communism) in the 20th century – it is
now the encompassing system worldwide[65,66,67]. So when we refer to the
Monetary System as it exists today we're essentially referring to
capitalism – the pre-eminent economic system.

2.3. How does the Monetary System function?

Money is created by Bank's then loaded out to people or institutions[68].

---

63 Graeber, David (2011). Debt: the first 5,000 years. New York: Melville House. pp. 40–41
64 D Kinley (2001). Money: A Study of the Theory of the Medium of Exchange. Simon Publications LLC,
1 September 2003
65 James Fulcher, Capitalism, A Very Short Introduction, p. 99, Oxford University Press, 2004
66http://www.academia.edu/4199690/Globalization_and_Economy_Vol._1_Global_Markets_and_Ca
pitalism_2007_
67 http://www.britannica.com/topic/capitalism
68 Abel, Andrew; Bernanke, Ben (2005). "7". Macroeconomics (5th ed.). Pearson. pp. 266–269

Every dollar in the world today originated as a loan. The modern Monetary System is a debt-based system and as we all know, with every debt there is interest. Interest is owed on top of the original money created[69]. This is the way it works in every country in the world today[70].

What does this debt-based money creation process imply? In the world today there's always more money owed in *debt plus interest repayments* than was originally created in *debt alone*. In other words: there's always more money owed than is available.

Analogy

Thousands of years ago – before the creation of money – people are stuck on a desert island. They each produce things for survival - one man fishes, one woman knits clothing, and so on. Inconveniently, they spend a lot of time negotiating trades.

Realising this is inefficient, one man devises a better system. We'll call him the banker. He gathers everyone together and hands out shells marked with special stamps. He gives 100 shells to each person and declares each shell worth one fish. The people could now exchange things directly without endless bartering. It made sense, everyone was sold on the idea.

The banker said the shells were a loan. In one year they'd have to pay back their 100 shells plus 10 more shells as a token of appreciation for the improvement he added to their lives. The people were puzzled. They asked how they could pay back more shells than were collectively given to them. The banker assured them they needn't worry, he would create even more shells next year.

This is a simplified analogy of the money creation process today. While in the real world there are other factors at play - such as the speed money changes hands and the handling of interest repayments – those factors don't resolve the central issue of more money being owed than is available. The only way to address this issue is to continually create more money. Growth – continuous and never-ending – is the basis of our

69 Mankiw, N. Gregory (2002). "Chapter 18: Money Supply and Money Demand". Macroeconomics (5th ed.). Worth.
70 Frederic S. Mishkin, Economics of Money, Banking and Financial Markets, 10th Edition. Prentice Hall 2012

modern Monetary System.

Growth – in the context of our Monetary System - means a growth in the money supply. This means a growth in the amount of money people are willing and able to borrow. In other words: growth means creating more things we can *charge money for* and just as importantly, more things we're *willing to pay money for*. Effectively, growth means more production and more consumption.

While in the big picture it's all about production and consumption, the production part is not something most us can relate to in our daily lives. We are consumers - we can all relate to that - but not producers. Why not? Today – as a by-product of sheer scale - most of us are now workers. For the most part, large corporations produce, while we work.

2.4. The requirement for scarcity

At first glance, a social system requiring growth sounds good. It seemingly incentivises us to produce more and more stuff meaning there's more and more stuff to go around, more stuff for us all to enjoy. Our common sense intuitions suggest we'll eventually produce so much stuff that we'll all be living like royalty. Unfortunately this isn't the case. In fact, that can never happen in the Monetary System. Why not?

While the Monetary System encourages more and more production, it only does so up to a point. There's no incentive to produce enough of something to make it abundant.

Case study

A woman plants an apple tree in her yard and starts selling apples. She sells 1,000 apples in the first year. Then she realises she can make more money if she plants another tree. She does. She sells 2,000 apples the next year. This logic continues to work until eventually there's too many apples and people aren't willing to pay as much for them. At this point an apple producer loses incentive to continue planting more apple trees.

Growth (people producing and consuming more and more stuff) is the objective but it can only be achieved within conditions of relative scarcity. The Monetary System requires infinite growth but in order to achieve that it also requires infinite scarcity.

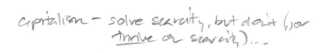

Case study

Diamonds are a scarce mineral with a high price in the Monetary System. If it rained diamonds for three hours we'd sweep them in our garage. We'd store them up in the knowledge we could sell them for a lot of money. What if it continued to rain diamonds for an entire year though? We'd probably start sweeping them out on the street. Diamonds would no longer be sought after, rather, they'd be a nuisance. They wouldn't be scarce, they'd be abundant. Nobody could charge money for them.[71]

Money is a medium of exchange. If things are abundant there's nothing to exchange. If things are abundant there's no way to earn money from them. Despite the buzzwords that exist, most things in the Monetary System can never be abundant, regardless if we have the capability to make them abundant (as we'll see later, we do).

If we stop and think about this situation, it isn't all that surprising. We know that money was created in conditions of scarcity specifically to manage those conditions of scarcity. It's not designed for conditions of abundance and as we've now seen, it's fundamentally incompatible with the idea of abundance.

Consequently, we're in the paradoxical situation of trying to eliminate scarcity from our world within the framework of a social system that actively requires scarcity. In other words: We're playing a game we can't win.

Quote

Charles Eisenstein – Author, Public Speaker

"Our perception of scarcity is a self-fulfilling prophecy. Money is central to the construction of the self-reifying illusion of scarcity. When everything is subject to money, then the scarcity of money makes everything scarce, including the basis of human life and happiness"

For the rest of this chapter we'll investigate the consequences of a society with a primary goal of growth that - as a result - also requires scarcity. The first consequence is widespread private ownership.

2.5. Ownership

---

71 http://www.thevenusproject.com/

We live in a society based on exchanging scarce resources - buying and selling things from one another. In order to do this we must own things. (Without ownership there could not be a Monetary System.) Even though we might not think of our lives as being immersed in ownership, it only takes a brief moment of introspection to appreciate the momentous influence it has in our day-to-day lives.

To get to work we gain ownership of fuel for our car or a public transport ticket; to look presentable at work we own clothes and other personal hygiene products; once at work our employer owns our time for the day; at work we use company property - our employer owns this stuff; at work we use electricity which our employer also owns; on our break we eat food and drink - we own these things, albeit momentarily until we consume them and convert them into energy; from our salary we pay taxes and gain ownership of our share of the policing, healthcare, justice, roading, and so on that our government provides.

There's not much left on Earth that hasn't been converted into something we can charge money for. Price tags have been added to things that never had a price tag in the past. From creative new service fees on event tickets, utility bills, or contracts, to things like childcare, music, television, knowledge, and opinions, right through to the most basic goods required for human survival like bottled water, and more recently, oxygen being sold in pubs and bars.[72,73,74]

What's the consequence of such pervasive ownership? When everything is owned by someone it means every time we need something we have to pay someone else for it, making goods and services scarce.) This consigns most of us to a life of limitation unnecessarily by limiting the breadth and quality of things we can each individually afford.

This limitation is not always obvious though because technology continually improves. Better technology means cooler stuff and cooler stuff makes it appear as though things are improving in our social world. They're not though. Our technology is producing bigger and better things but our social system's requirement for widespread private ownership is severely restricting our ability to enjoy them. It's critical we understand

72 http://business.time.com/2013/02/20/youll-never-guess-what-banks-have-started-charging-for-now/
73 http://storyofstuff.org/movies/story-of-bottled-water/
74 http://en.wikipedia.org/wiki/Oxygen_bar

this distinction between improving technology (which will always happen) and an improving social system (which is not happening)[75].

The idea of gaining ownership of something then selling that thing to others is really quite primitive. It's grounded in a social system devoid of trust and compassion where it's everyone for themselves[76]. A system of money breeds a culture of widespread private ownership which ensures we continue to suffer in conditions of scarcity.

2.6. Work

Today we work, in order to earn money, in order to survive[77]. We each must individually work so we can earn money for ourselves and provide for ourselves. With so much of our lives and thoughts overwhelmed by work, few of us question the suitability of our society - one in which we have so many advanced technologies and capabilities (this will be covered in detail in Chapter 5) yet we still must individually work in order to survive. This situation of working to survive is akin to slavery. This contemporary form of systemic slavery is formidable in that most people don't see themselves as slaves.

Every country in the world today blindly strives for full employment. We don't question the value of each job, all that matters is we're employed. We don't stop to consider how much work needs to be done or what kind of work needs to be done in order to create a world we want to live in. We just work, incredibly hard.

While hard work can indeed be rewarding, it's only rewarding if it's *worth doing*. This is the critical piece. As we'll see in Chapter 6, the majority of the work in the Monetary System is not worth doing, nor does it motivate us.

The type of work we do today is highly specialised. Regardless of our field, most of us do a specific task which we make a career of. Why is this? Because if we all new a little about a lot we wouldn't have the advanced civilisation we do today. We've been able to advance because we've

---

75 http://www.businesswire.com/news/home/20070426005614/en/Average-U.S.-Household-50-Unused-Items-Worth#.VNgf3vnF-So

76 http://www.indiana.edu/~workshop/publications/materials/W11-15_BlancoEtAl.pdf

77 http://www2.hn.psu.edu/faculty/jmanis/adam-smith/wealth-nations.pdf

specialised then co-operated to share that knowledge.

Case study
No individual could build a jumbo jet. The level of knowledge required across all aspects of aircraft design is more than one person could know. You need a group of people with specific knowledge, from mechanical engineering, to aerodynamics, to cabin pressurisation, to electronics, to welding and custom fabrication, to spatial planning, to food preparation, to plumbing, to flight planning, to logistics, and so on.

Specialisation is a by-product of a civilisation becoming more advanced[78]. As civilisations become more advanced they use increasing levels of specialisation to elevate the standard of living. Unfortunately, with increased specialisation usually comes increased repetition. This makes the average job menial and unenjoyable.

Research
Global studies across 140 countries over the past few years repeatedly show just over 10% of people actually enjoy their jobs[79]. The overwhelming majority of us are spending most of our lives forced to work hard at something we don't enjoy. It's turning us into unhappy, unproductive, and unmotivated human beings.[80,81,82]

It doesn't have to be this way though. We don't have to be just another barcode punching a clock. We can have an advanced civilisation without being consigned to a life of specialised and unenjoyable work. We'll look at this in detail in Chapter 6.

Today we're told we should "work to live, not live to work". This is a nice saying but it's just hot air. We spend 50 years – almost our entire adult lives - working five days on, two days off, doing something we don't even enjoy (for 90% of us). On our two days off we scamper round trying to organise everything: do the shopping, pay the bills, clean the house, clean the car, do the gardening, do the laundry, and so on. How much time do

78 http://jmcentarfer.tripod.com/ch1_3.pdf
79 http://www.gallup.com/strategicconsulting/164735/state-global-workplace.aspx
80 http://www2.warwick.ac.uk/knowledge/business/productivity/#.U3b38vmSzwh
81http://www.businessweek.com/debateroom/archives/2012/02/employee_happiness_matters_mo re_than_you_think.html
82 http://www.nytimes.com/2011/09/04/opinion/sunday/do-happier-people-work-harder.html?_r=2&

we really have to live?

Quote
Johann Wolfgang von Goethe – Scientist, Philosopher
"None are more hopelessly enslaved than those who falsely believe they are free"

2.7. Competition

Competition is the next consequence of the way our social system is structured. As we clamour for our share of the scarce resources, competition becomes a way of life. (Unfortunately, we're biologically reliant on co-operation (because most of the development of our brain happens after birth – it is not innate). We're critically dependent on co-operation yet we've created a society exquisitely dependent on competition.

In a society based on scarcity, every institution is in competition with one another. Countries compete for resources, corporations compete for profit, and people compete for jobs. Everyone is looking out for their own and nobody is looking out for the whole. Consequently, if there's a problem that needs to be solved but there's no way to profit from solving the problem, the problem will not be solved.

Case study
We have a water shortage. There's 800 million people without access to clean water. For decades we've had the technological capability to produce an endless supply of clean water (we'll cover this in Chapter 5). We know how to solve the water shortage but we don't know how to profit from solving the water shortage. Consequently, the problem remains unresolved.

Water is one example but as we'll see in Chapter 5, we have the technological capability today to solve every major problem we face. The problems don't get solved though, not because we can't solve them but because we can't profit from them. That's the way it's always been and will always be in a monetary social system based on growth and scarcity.

2.8. Waste

In a social system based on growth, we continually produce more and more stuff. Whether we like it or not though, the resources available to produce this stuff are not infinite. We've created a social system that requires infinite growth on a finite planet.

The Earth is 4.6 billion years old. If we scale that down from 4.6 billion years to 4.6 years (a timeframe we can relate to), our modern capitalist society has been running the show for the last 6 seconds of that time. In that incredibly brief instant of the Earth's history we've:[83,84,85,86,87,88,89]

- Lost a third of the arable land through soil erosion
- Destroyed half of the forests - critical for the life-supporting balance of our atmosphere
- Over-exploited or depleted 85% of global fish stocks
- Caused 20% of drylands to suffer desertification - becoming arid and lifeless
- Pumped water from rivers faster than rainfall can replenish
- Leached half of the topsoil
- Been destroying wildlife habitats and as a result we've seen a 50% decline in mammals, birds, reptiles, and amphibians over the last 40 years.

It doesn't take a mathematician to realise this isn't sustainable. We have finite natural resources and in the infinitely growing Monetary System these are being used at an accelerated rate[90,91,92,93].

Most of us are now aware of the materialistic, consumer culture that's feeding this. The throw-away culture is nobody's fault though. It's a result of corporations trying to find a way to meet ever-increasing profit targets (a product of a social system based on growth, scarcity, and

83 http://consensusforaction.stanford.edu/see-scientific-consensus/consensus_english.pdf
84 http://www.worldwildlife.org/threats/soil-erosion-and-degradation
85 http://www.ecologyandsociety.org/vol14/iss2/art32/
86 http://www.worldwildlife.org/threats/deforestation
87http://wwf.panda.org/about_our_Earth/top_5_environmental_questions/top_5_questions_about_forests/
88 http://www.worldwildlife.org/pages/living-planet-report-2014?amp&amp
89 http://books.google.ca/books?id=XxBrq6hTs_UC&pg=PA454&redir_esc=y#v=onepage&q&f=false
90 http://rspb.royalsocietypublishing.org/content/280/1754/20122845.full.pdf+html
91 Rees WE. In press. Ecological footprint, concept of. In Encyclopedia of biodiversity (ed. S Levin), 2nd edn. San Diego, CA: Academic Press
92 Wackernagel M, Rees W. 1996 Our ecological footprint: reducing human impact on the Earth. Gabriola Island, BC: New Society Publishers
93 Global Footprint Network 2012 World footprint: do we fit the planet. See http://www.footprintnetwork.org/en/index.php/GFN/page/world_footprint/

competition)[94]. As a result, products have become cheaper[95], designed to break more quickly[96,97,98,99], and engineered to be re-purchased within a relatively short period of time[100,101,102,103]. Of the products flowing through our consumer society today, only 1% remain in use 6 months after sale[104]. This gross over-consumption is rendered so normal by advertising and media that we hardly notice how wasteful we've become.

While not all economic growth necessarily requires us to waste resources, the type of growth we're experiencing today most certainly does[105,106]. While this was once tin-foil hat stuff, it has become common knowledge. Based on current trends of exploitation, depletion, and degradation - by 2050 we may need up to 27 Earth's to support the projected 10 billion people[107].

Quote
Carl Sagan - Cosmologist

"We ravage the Earth at an accelerated pace as if it belonged to this one generation – as if it were ours to do with as we please. Our generation must choose, which do we value more, short term profits or the long term habitability of our planetary home. The world is divided politically but ecologically it is tightly interwoven. There are no useless threads in the fabric of the ecosystem – if you cut any one of them you will unravel many others. The Earth has mechanisms to neutralise itself but these mechanisms work only up to a point. Beyond some critical threshold they

---

94 Babaian, Sharon (1998). The Most Benevolent Machine: A Historical Assessment of Cycles in Canada. National Museum of Science and Technology (Ottawa). p. 97.ISBN 0-660-91670-3.
95 http://faculty-gsb.stanford.edu/bulow/articles/An%20Economic%20Theory%20of%20Planned%20Obsolescence.pdf
96 http://www.computerworld.com/article/2512542/computer-hardware/gadgets--built-to-not-last.html
97 http://www.economist.com/node/13354332
98 http://bankrupt.com/CAR_Public/040816.mbx
99 http://www.hup.harvard.edu/catalog.php?isbn=9780674025721
100 "Idea: Planned obsolescence". The Economist. March 25, 2009
101 The Shady World of Repair Manuals: Copyrighting for Planned Obsolescence | Wired Opinion | Wired.com
102 https://www.aeaweb.org/assa/2005/0107_1015_0616.pdf
103 http://mitpress.mit.edu/books/industrial-strength-design
104 http://storyofstuff.org/
105 http://www.pnas.org/content/112/20/6271.full
106 http://www.sciencedirect.com/science/article/pii/S0959378012001501
107http://share.disl.org/heck/advanced%20marine%20ecology/Shared%20Documents/Mora%20and%20Sale%202011%20MEPS,%20marine%20reserves(Background).pdf

break down – the damage becomes irreversible. This is not a disposable
planet and we are not yet able to re-engineer other planets"

Our social system has us racing to consume every resource possible until
there are none left to survive. Unfortunately, without resources it won't
matter how much money we have. We can't eat money, can't drink
money, can't power our cars with money, can't heat our homes with
money, and can't build infrastructure with money.

Reading about the current resource depletion scares us but it's not
particularly noticeable in our daily lives. From our day-to-day experience
we seem to have access to everything we need right now. We hit the light
switch and the light turns on, we go to the supermarket and the food is on
the shelf, we go to the gas station and fuel comes out the pump.
Psychologically we find it difficult to perceive a problem until there
already is one.[108]

What does all this mean? Do we need to cut back to a basic lifestyle to be
sustainable? No, we don't. Complete resource depletion is far from an
inevitability. We're also developing new technologies that can sustainably
produce an abundance of resources and halt the current ecological
degradation. We just have to change the way we produce, distribute, and
use our stuff. With a more efficient approach we could have everything
we do today but without destroying the planet we depend on to stay
alive. We'll cover this in detail in Chapters 5 and 6.

2.9. Inequality

Inequality is a by-product of a social system that requires us to compete
for scarce resources. Over the past two centuries it's become increasingly
worse. The income gap between the richest 20% of countries and the
poorest 20% of countries:

- in 1800 was 3:1
- in 1960 was 30:1
- In 1998 was 74:1
- And today, it's 80:1[109]

competition ⇆ inequality

---

108 http://www.thelancet.com/journals/lancet/article/PIIS0140-6736(15)60901-1/abstract
109 http://hdr.undp.org/en/reports/global/hdr1999

It's reached a point where we now have some absurd situations: Firstly, the richest 200 people in the world have the same amount of money as the poorest 3.5 billion people combined (almost half of all humans on the planet).[110] Secondly, Exxon Mobil (the U.S oil company) makes more revenue each year than Libya, Uruguay, Syria, Serbia, Cameroon, Paraguay, Ivory Coast, Afghanistan, Congo, North Korea, Senegal, Iceland, and Albania combined[111,112,113]. How does all this inequality affect us?

Research

A study of over 50,000 U.S households between 1972 – 2008 showed that while average incomes had almost doubled[114], people had not become happier. (People were happiest in times of relative income equality.) There was no correlation between happiness and gross incomes. The strong correlation was between unhappiness and inequality, whereby greater inequality led to lower levels of perceived fairness and trust which would disjoint and divide communities, further reducing happiness[115].

Studies into the effects of inequality around the world are coming to the same conclusions: (Greater inequality equates to lower levels of social mobility, trust, economic growth, community life, physical health, life expectancy, educational performance, and innovation.) At the same time, greater inequality also leads to higher levels of obesity, drug abuse, violence, teenage births, and rates of imprisonment[116].

2.10. Poverty

The inbuilt inequality and scarcity lead to poverty. This is known as structural violence.

Quote
Paul Farmer – Anthropologist, Physician
"Structural violence is one way of describing social arrangements that put individuals and populations in harm's way.. The arrangements are structural because they're embedded in the political and economic

110 http://www.therules.org/en/inequality-video-fact-sheet;
111 http://www.moneymeters.org/
112 https://www.google.com/finance?q=NYSE:XOM&fstype=ii&ei=61EXU7iCB8r_kAX7-wE
113 http://en.wikipedia.org/wiki/List_of_countries_by_population
114 http://www.epi.org/publication/the_state_of_working_americas_wealth_2011/
115 http://pss.sagepub.com/content/22/9/1095.abstract
116 http://inequality.org/inequality-health/

organisation of our social world, they're violent because they cause injury to people.. neither culture nor pure individual will is at fault. Structural violence is visited upon all those whose social status denies them access to the fruits of scientific and social progress"

The Monetary System is the social structure that harms billions of people by unnecessarily preventing them from meeting their basic needs. Structural violence doesn't have a face or a name nor does it come with an exciting story. There often isn't a villain or hero so we barely hear about it in the news. With nobody to blame, structural violence is passed off as an unfortunate situation. We become desensitised to it.

Case study

When a Peruvian shantytown burns, people lose what little they owned. Some of them burn alive from a fire started due to improvised and unventilated indoor cooking. A local fire department doesn't exist because this shantytown is decades away from the infrastructure that much of the developed world enjoys. Did the shantytown kill them? The lack of a fire department? The improvised indoor cooking? There is no clear villain in this complex situation but the harm is there and it is structural violence.[117,118]

So who is the villain? It's the Monetary System with its inbuilt, unnecessary, and widespread poverty. It's causing more harm than all of the serial killers, warlords, terrorists, dictators, and despotic regimes ever did.

The most destructive thing happening in our world today (the structural violence of the Monetary System) is not the most intuitively disturbing though. Warlords who torture women and children are more intuitively disturbing so we're more aware of them than we are of structural violence. Structural violence is a far more devastating problem for humanity in the big picture though.

Those who suffer from poverty is largely pre-determined

Who are the poor people that suffer from poverty? And why are they poor? Are they stupid? Are they bad people who don't deserve access to

117 http://www.structuralviolence.org/structural-violence/
118 https://www.youtube.com/watch?v=QMUhLGUP_pE

the resources the wealthy have?

There are over 7 billion of us on Earth and our station in life is determined by the luck of the draw in some sort of birth lottery - how few options we have, what government we contribute to, what economic system we use, how we're educated, what religion we're taught, and so on. It's like a really bad game of Monopoly, where by the time you join the game, somebody else has all the properties.[119]

For most of us, our status today is more or less the same as it was at birth. Yes, rags to riches stories do happen but they're the exception, not the norm. There is an 80% correlation between the level of wealth we're born into and the level of wealth we enjoy as adults[120].

For most of us, the decisions we make in life alter our status slightly but not much. Research shows we don't like to accept this. We tend to turn a blind eye to the situational advantages that got us to where we are today.

Research

Two strangers play a game of monopoly. The game is heavily rigged - one player starts with more money and collects more money each time they pass go. The flip of a coin determines which player gains the advantage. Almost every time, the player who won the flip of the coin wins the game. After each game the players are interviewed. When the winners evaluate the game, they focus on their strategies and key moves. They're quick to forget the toss of the coin that gave them the almost unbeatable situational advantage.[121]

Why don't we admit to these situational advantages? Well, the thought that blind luck is the reason we're sitting in our modern house and not a mud hut is pretty scary. The thought we've worked hard to earn our modern conveniences is far more comforting, reassuring, and rewarding, so we go with that. Maybe you've worked hard and made good decisions but if you lucked out in the birth lottery and were born in a shantytown you'd probably still be there or thereabouts.

2.11. Summary

unequal origins = rigged.

119 http://www.abiggishidea.com/
120 https://www.youtube.com/watch?v=hchXtBPSAZ4
121 http://www.ted.com/talks/paul_piff_does_money_make_you_mean

We've now covered a relatively simplified high-level view of the way our social system works. Below is a visual representation of the implications of a society with a primary goal of growth – one in which to achieve that goal we must also have conditions of relative scarcity.

Having growth and scarcity embedded in the fabric of our social system leads to inherent ownership, work, competition, waste, inequality, and poverty. There's no rules or laws specifically dictating these things must happen. They're natural by-products of the structure of the social system.

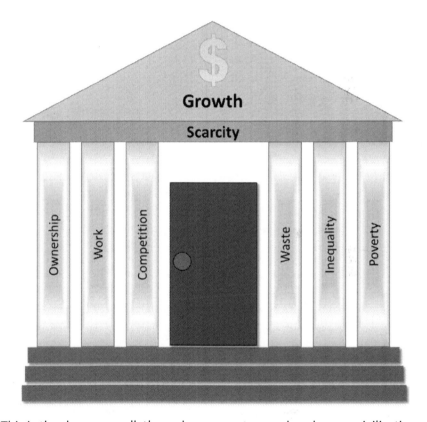

This is the door we walk through as we enter modern human civilisation, regardless of our race, country, or religion. This is the world we live in.

2.12. Who's responsible for this mess?

We know that Bank's *create* money, but who *manages* money as a tool of social organisation? Who assesses the suitability of money as a social system?

The short answer is nobody. Today there are 180 monetary currencies across 198 countries and over 100 million corporations[122,123]. While some people wield enormous power and influence within the system – such as those issuing the currencies – no one person or group of people has any controlled or co-ordinated stewardship over money as our system of social organisation.

There's many conspiracy theories that romanticise about an elite group of people at the top with hidden agenda's, exploiting the rest of us for their own benefit. Some of the more well-known revolve around the Rothschild's, the Illuminati or New World Order, and the Bilderberg Group[124,125,126]. Whether these conspiracies are true or not is outside the scope of this book though. Whether or not they're true does not impact on the fundamental structural organisation of our social system based on money. Our social system – and the mechanics of that system - was there long before any of the people or groups within it today.

While there are undoubtedly some corrupt, greedy, and unsavoury individuals in our world today, these individuals are not the cause of our problems. Our problems are systemic. Yes, we created money, and yes, there are some very powerful people using it to significantly influence society, but like us they are a symptom of the inhumanity of our Monetary System, not a cause of the inhumanity of our Monetary System.

So if there's no leaders of money itself, who ensures the required conditions of constant growth within conditions of relative scarcity are maintained? We all do. Growth and scarcity are naturally maintained through everyone simply – and not maliciously - looking out for their own interests. Growth takes care of itself through the systemic need for each individual, corporation, and country to earn as much money as possible to improve their own lives. It is a particularly unvirtuous cycle.

Money is self-fulfilling and self-perpetuating and with it so are the

---

122 http://en.wikipedia.org/wiki/List_of_circulating_currencies
123 http://www.ifc.org/wps/wcm/connect/9ae1dd80495860d6a482b519583b6d16/MSME-CI-AnalysisNote.pdf?MOD=AJPERES
124 http://www.conspiracytruths.co.uk/rothschilds.html
125 http://www.trueconspiracies.com/
126 http://www.globalresearch.ca/the-true-story-of-the-bilderberg-group-and-what-they-may-be-planning-now/13808

conditions of scarcity we experience today. Money is a dynamic, complex, fluid entity unto itself. It proliferates a civilisation that is unintentionally harmful to itself.

3. HOW HAS MONEY SHAPED US?

3.1. Introduction

Quote
Jacque Fresco – Futurist
"The sunflower does not turn to the sun, the sun makes it turn. The
sailboat cannot sail, the wind moves it. Plants can't grow, they're shoved
by sunshine and soil. All things are pushed by something else. All people
are acted upon by other things"

Human behaviour does not occur in a vacuum. Much like everything else
in nature, our behaviour is driven by the symbiotic relationship we have
with everything around us. Despite what many of us feel, we are not the
ultimate masters of our destiny, the sole authors of our decisions, or the
principal architects of our thoughts. We are indeed amazing creatures but
we're amazing creatures at the mercy of our environment rather than
amazing creatures in charge of our environment.

There is enormous scope for both good and bad in human nature. In this
chapter we'll investigate the underlying characteristics of our nature the
Monetary System promotes. These aren't characteristics we all exhibit all
the time, just ones most of us exhibit most of the time. We'll see that
much of the bad in human nature today is not innate or absolute, rather,
it's a product of the social system that conditions our nature.

We know our brains are built on the fly in response to our environment.
How is our environment programming our brains today? What
behaviours, values, and beliefs are encouraged today through our cultural
immersion in the Monetary System?

3.2. Self-interested

With inherent scarcity in our social system, we must look out for ourselves
first. If we don't, we may not get enough of the scarce resources to
survive and prosper. While focusing on ourselves is a basic survival
instinct, the extent we do this can vary greatly. We have a marvellous
plasticity of mind – we can be incredibly selfish sometimes and endlessly
altruistic other times.

Research
Fifteen experimental small-scale societies were created across twelve
countries on four continents. The societies were created with a wide
variety of economic and social systems. The experiment tested if we're
always self-interested, regardless of the social situation. It turned out the
level of selfishness or altruism depended on which behaviours were
promoted by the social system.[127]

Many of us despair today at the selfishness we see around us. We lament
this unfortunate condition of human nature. As the study above
demonstrates though, selfishness is not innate in human nature. Yes, it's a
big part of human nature within the Monetary System, but it is not human
nature per se. Through a scarce, competitive, dog-eat-dog social system, it
has just *temporarily become human nature*[128].

With the overwhelming focus on self-interest, self-preservation, and self-
maximisation, many of us lack a broader perspective about our social
world. We understand how money works for us but we don't understand
how money works.

Quote
Adam Smith – Father of modern economics
"It is not from the benevolence of the butcher, the brewer, or the baker
that we expect our dinner, but from their regard to their own interest"

We've created a society that continues to function as a by-product of
everyone looking out for themselves. While it works relatively effectively
compared to say, Barter, or other more primitive social systems, it isn't
effective at all when we compare it to what it could be. This will become
clear in later chapters.

3.3. Afraid

When we have a scarce and unequal society we become afraid of not
getting enough and we become afraid of the agendas of others. We don't
all think of it this way because we've become accustomed to it – it's just
life - but it doesn't take too much introspection to appreciate the fear-

---

127 http://authors.library.caltech.edu/2278/1/HENbbs05.pdf
128 http://www.sciencemag.org/content/314/5802/1154.full

based society we live in.

The people in poverty are constantly afraid of hunger, malnutrition, and all sorts of diseases. Most of the middle class now live week to week and are so financially reliant on their menial jobs that they're afraid to follow their dreams. And even the rich are afraid, of being robbed or attacked by the poor, so they spend inordinate amounts of money building fences around their sprawling mansions. Wars are perpetual as countries fear not getting the resources they need to sustain their way of life, and with everyone out for themselves, things like terrorism, organised crime, government spying, and religious extremism are rife in all corners of the world.

It doesn't have to be this way. While fear is a natural biological emotion, it's more pervasive than it needs to be as a result of living in a world of widespread scarcity and inequality. When there isn't enough for everyone and we have to compete to survive, we naturally fear not getting enough of the scarce resources for ourselves.

Even though we don't always admit it, fear grips us. Fear means we accept our boring menial jobs and the police state of rules that control us. It prevents us challenging the status quo, inhibits our enjoyment of life, and smothers our full potential. This reality will become strikingly apparent as we investigate the ways an alternative social system might shape us in Chapter 8.

3.4. Greedy

When our society has inbuilt requirements for growth, competition, and self-interest, an intense desire for wealth and power is encouraged. What happens as our greedy desires deliver increasing wealth? Excessive wealth is continually shown to lead to feelings of self-entitlement and self-importance, a lack of compassion for others, and a willingness to cheat, lie, and break rules for personal gain.[129,130,131,132,133]

We've created a society that encourages us to strive for as much money

129 http://greatergood.berkeley.edu/article/item/the_poor_give_more
130 http://philanthropy.com/article/America-s-Generosity-Divide/133775/
131 http://www.sciencemag.org/content/341/6149/976
132 http://www.ncbi.nlm.nih.gov/pubmed/20974714
133 http://www.pnas.org/content/early/2012/02/21/1118373109.full.pdf+html

as possible - to be "successful". Unfortunately, studies continually show the more successful we become in this system, the more we diminish our ability to be decent human beings. Our definition of success is warped. Success in the Monetary System leads to a failure in values and behaviour.

There is no upper limit to success and consequently no upper limit to how much wealth we can acquire. Our cultural aspiration for increasing wealth leaves us like junkies clucking for a fix that we can never get enough of but always want more of.

The limitless goal of acquiring wealth is the primary yardstick for measuring people[134]. Unfortunately, studies continue to show there is no correlation between having lots of wealth and being happy. In fact, beyond a certain level there is a negative correlation[135,136]. The Monetary System's yardstick for success appears to disagree with human physiology on a fundamental level[137]. With more wealth comes more power. How does power affect us?

Powerful people experience a positive internal response from lying and can do so without displaying the expected physiological tell-tale signs. In other words, becoming powerful biologically enhances us to lie, cheat, and steal[138]. Powerful people are also more hypocritical – they're willing to bend the rules while at the same time they're harsher on others for bending the rules. Power breeds a sense of self-entitlement[139]. Power also leads to a lack of compassion for others, with powerful people experiencing lower levels of distress when confronted with another's suffering. They also have a weaker desire to form relationships with others[140].

These findings raise doubts about the appropriateness of a hierarchical society that encourages us all to seek power and allows an incredibly

---

134http://www.jstor.org/discover/10.1086/680087?uid=3739448&uid=2&uid=3737720&uid=4&sid=2 1106053593063

135 Cummins, R. A. (2000). Personal income and subjective well-being: A review. Journal of Happiness Studies, 1, 133–158

136 Suh, E., Diener, E., Oishi, S., & Triandis, H. C. (1998). The shifting basis of life satisfaction judgments across cultures: Emotions versus norms. Journal of Personality and Social Psychology, 74, 482–493.

137 Diener, E., & Seligman, M. E. P. (2004). Beyond money: Toward an economy of well-being. Psychological Science in the Public Interest, 5, 1–31

138 http://www.academia.edu/306700/People_With_Power_Are_Better_Liars

139 http://pss.sagepub.com/content/21/5/737.abstract

140 http://www.psychologicalscience.org/media/releases/2008/vankleef.cfm

small minority of extremely powerful leaders to determine our future. Despite this, almost every industry in the world is consolidating power, from banking[141,142], to pharmaceuticals[143], to oil & rail[144], to airlines[145], to music[146], to automotive[147], to agriculture[148], and many more.

Quote

Abraham Lincoln – Former President of the United States
"Nearly all men can stand adversity. If you want to test a man's character, give him power"

Our greedy, power-driven society lends itself to corrupt behaviour. Corruption is an abuse of entrusted power for private gain. It's estimated to be worth about 5% of Global GDP[149]. Most people think of corruption as something that only occurs in 3rd world countries but that couldn't be further from the truth. In the 20 years from 1993 to 2012 there were 20,294 U.S government officials convicted of corruption.[150]

That is a lot of corruption, but keep in mind, the number above is only those actually convicted of corruption, we don't know about the many who got away with it. Furthermore, the number above is only government officials, it doesn't account for business and corporate corruption. Further still, the number above is only in the U.S, just one of 198 countries and certainly not a 3rd world country with an image of having a corrupt government.

Greed and corruption are by-products of a hierarchical social system with an overwhelming focus on self-interest and inbuilt requirements for growth and competition. An abundance of psychology research demonstrates that greed is inherent in the Monetary System but not necessarily in human nature (such as the Christmas study and small-scale

---

141 http://research.stlouisfed.org/publications/review/11/11/419-438Wheelock.pdf
142 http://www.fdic.gov/bank/analytical/banking/2006jan/article2/article2.pdf
143http://www.sauder.ubc.ca/Faculty/Research_Centres/ISIS/Resources/~/media/7362023FB3DF40
DF8CB8D9A6DF3CC533.ashx
144 http://mba.tuck.dartmouth.edu/pdf/2002-1-0073.pdf
145 http://www.airlines.org/Pages/U.S.-Airline-Mergers-and-Acquisitions.aspx
146 http://www.nytimes.com/2011/11/12/business/media/emi-is-sold-for-4-1-billion-consolidating-the-music-industry.html?_r=0
147 https://gsbapps.stanford.edu/cases/documents/EC10.pdf
148 http://www.foodtechconnect.com/site/wp-content/uploads/2011/12/cows1.jpg
149http://web.worldbank.org/WBSITE/EXTERNAL/NEWS/0,,contentMDK:20190295~menuPK:34457~
pagePK:34370~piPK:34424~theSitePK:4607,00.html
150 http://www.justice.gov/criminal/pin/docs/2012-Annual-Report.pdf

societies study, among many others).

3.4. Materialistic

In a greedy society based on growth, scarcity, and ownership, we tend to be overly materialistic. When the material things we own determine our quality of life, we naturally end up measuring personal success by those very material things – nice car, nice house, shiny things, the person is successful[151]. In some cases we even end up loving our things more than we love each other. This materialistic culture becomes firmly entrenched in most of us from a young age.

Case study
Some of our first memories are of Birthdays and Christmas time. We receive material gifts and learn to measure the value of our relationship with a person by the quality of the gift. The better the gift, the more important the person is to us (e.g. the best gifts come from parents, lesser gifts from uncles and aunties, and even lesser gifts from 2nd cousins)[152]. One of the first questions we're asked as children that really fires our imagination is "What do you want for Christmas?". It is here we begin to fantasise about what we can and could acquire.

Material things have become a measuring stick for our status as much as something that actually provides genuine enjoyment[153]. Unfortunately, being measured chiefly by our stuff compromises our values and psychologically damages us[154]. That's because it doesn't matter how great our own stuff is, there's always someone else with bigger and better stuff. This leaves many of us permanently disillusioned and discontented with our lives and the stuff we own[155].

Money – if we have enough of it - enables us to buy any material thing we desire. This makes us feel entitled, so much so that the resulting degradation of the Earth – our only habitable home - goes seemingly unnoticed. That's because the only narrative we're really made aware of

151 Robert Brym; John Lie (11 June 2009). Sociology: Your Compass for a New World, Brief Edition: Enhanced Edition. Cengage Learning. p. 88
152 Pierce, J. L.; Kostova, T.; Dirks, K. T. (2003). "The state of psychological ownership: integrating and extending a century of research". Review of General Psychology 7: 84–107
153 http://pss.sagepub.com/content/early/2014/08/21/0956797614546556.abstract?rss=1#aff-1
154 http://esr.oxfordjournals.org/content/30/2/151.abstract.html?etoc
155 http://time.com/22257/heres-proof-buying-more-stuff-actually-makes-you-miserable/

is if we work hard and earn enough money we'll be entitled to use resources, animals, and people to our benefit, almost ad libitum.

Too often today material things are loved and people are used. It should be the other way around. This is not necessarily an inherent failure in human nature though. It's reflective of our social system based on growth, scarcity, and ownership.

3.5. Robotic

When we have a society with an inbuilt requirement for specialised work, we're naturally shaped to enable us to endure specialised work. We're largely shaped in regimented schools during our developmental years:

- Show up every morning wearing a specific uniform
- Have our shirts tucked in, socks pulled up, shoes shined, hair tidy
- Learn a number of different subjects at prescribed times
- Eat when we're told, regardless of whether we're hungry
- Never question our teachers orders, even if they don't make sense

Quote
Albert Einstein - Nobel Prize winning theoretical physicist
"It is a miracle that curiosity survives formal education"

We recite facts, formulas, and procedures in order to come to an answer but we're only sparsely taught genuine cognitive skills such as inferring, analysing, evaluating, justifying, categorising, and decoding[156]. We learn to pass exams rather than to think for ourselves. We're subjected to a stifling bombardment of largely meaningless information[157,158].

There's an idealistic notion that we go to school to learn about the world. The truth is we go to school to be groomed for work and evaluated on how well we might be able to work. Instead of educating people we train them to get jobs. The unfortunate externality of training people to work is that imagination, creativity, and intellectual potential are suffocated.

---

156 http://www.press.uchicago.edu/ucp/books/book/chicago/A/bo10327226.html
157 http://www.iflscience.com/how-teach-all-students-think-critically
158 http://assessment.aas.duke.edu/documents/Delphi_Report.pdf

Quote
Carl Sagan – Cosmologist
"Every one of us begins life with an open mind, a driving curiosity, a sense of wonder. When you go and talk to 1st grade students they ask deep questions – Why do we dream? Why do we have toes? Why is the moon round? What's the birthday of the world? Why is grass green? These are profound important questions that just bubble right out of them. When you go and talk to 12th grade students you get none of that. They've become leaden and incurious. Something terrible has happened"

Research
This study tests our creative and interpretive ability to see many different answers to a question. The study asks questions such as "how many uses can you think of for a paper clip?" Most people come up with 10 to 15. People at genius level for this type of creative thinking come up with around 200. A longitudinal study of kindergarten children measured 98% of them at genius level. Five years later those at genius level had dropped to 50%. By the time they were teenagers those at genius level had fallen further still.[159]

We're all born with tremendous imaginative and creative capabilities but these diminish as we grow up today. In schools we're told the answers, they're at the back of the book. We're not encouraged to question existing knowledge, we're just required to recite the things our teachers tell us.

It only takes a brief moment of introspection to realise how incurious most of us have become today. We gorge on fiction, whether it be a novel, TV series, or movie. Very few of us choose to learn deeply about a new field of knowledge and fewer still keep up with the latest discoveries in science. Our voracious appetite for learning – something we were all born with – has seemingly vanished. By the end of our education (where we're forced to learn dry and boring content for 12 years) the act of learning has become an exhausting chore for most. While some of this may be an evolutionary trait of growing up, our monetary and educational system undoubtedly exacerbate the situation.

The common rhetoric today is that work keeps our brain active, keeps us challenged, and without it we'd be bored and struggle to fill our days.

159 http://jrs.sagepub.com/content/104/10/391

Most adults no longer have the capacity to thrive on self-directed creative, educational, and leisure pursuits, despite existing on a planet bursting with wonders to stimulate the mind and body. Today most adults without work default to a state of stale lethargy and apathy. This is a scathing indictment on the way we've been conditioned to rely on others to tell us what to do. When children grow up being told the answers rather than being encouraged to ask questions, they turn into adults that struggle to objectively assess the situations they face.

Research

The volunteer in this study is asked to teach another person a list of word pairs. They're also instructed to administer an electric shock to the other person each time they answer a word pair incorrectly. After each incorrect answer they must administer a greater shock, until they reach a final 450 volt potentially lethal shock. They can't see the other person because they're in a separate room but they can hear their screams of pain each time they administer the shock. In reality there is no shock actually given (the screams are fake) but the volunteer doesn't know this. If the volunteer gets uncomfortable at any stage and requests to stop the experiment they're told by the researcher that they "must continue". Most of the time the volunteer goes all the way to the end, administering a potentially lethal electric shock to another human being simply because the researcher told them they had to.[160]

This study has been repeated with similar results around the world. It demonstrates the extent we robotically do as we're told – even into adulthood – with a startling inability to gauge the fundamental morality of our decisions.

Once we finish school we're akin to robots. Unfortunately, we're not cool robots with poly-metal skin or eyes that shoot laser beams. We're robotic in the sense we work and consume but just as importantly, in the sense we don't question what we're doing and raise our kids to do the same. This robotic production line of our education system continues to flourish through everyone simply wanting the best for their children. It's not malicious and it's not our fault. We put our kids in regimented schools because it gives them the best chance of prospering in the future of specialised work that awaits them.

---

160 http://www.cnr.berkeley.edu/ucce50/ag-labor/7article/article35.htm

3.6. Ignorant

Almost all of us have a basic awareness of the types of issues that exist today - from poverty to corruption to homelessness and so on. It's not a pretty picture though so most of us don't burden ourselves thinking too much about it. Instead we try to distance ourselves from society's problems. We focus on ourselves rather than our society. We seek to create a life for ourselves that we can be proud of - our energies are directed inward.

The Monetary System encourages this insular focus. That's because it doesn't matter if the rest of the world is in turmoil, if we have enough money individually we'll be able to afford the things we need and want. Our society impacts our quality of life less than our individual bank accounts do. As such, it's not surprising we're more personally, intellectually, and emotionally invested in our individual earnings than we are in our society's functioning.

Research
This study surveys many different subsets of the population on questions relating to the state of society. Not just any questions though, questions that critically underlie the way society is functioning today (stuff we should all know). For each question there are only three multiple choice answers to choose from. Each possible answer is wildly different to the others so anyone getting it wrong grossly misunderstands the reality of the situation. In all subsets of the survey (media, businesspeople, politicians, average citizens, etc), the majority of people get it wrong, far more than would be expected even if they just made their picks at random.[161]

With a widespread ignorance about the way the world works, we end up inheriting very different opinions and beliefs. We usually develop our opinions from the family and community we grow up in and they become ensconced in the fabric of our personalities.

Thought experiment
The first major opinion/belief most of us learn is a religion. There are an estimated 4,000 religious beliefs in the world[162]. Christianity – one of

---

161https://www.ted.com/talks/hans_and_ola_rosling_how_not_to_be_ignorant_about_the_world?language=en
162 The Everything World's Religions Book: Explore the Beliefs, Traditions and Cultures of Ancient and

those 4,000 – has an estimated 42,000 sub-branches[163]. So many confident religious ideologies - confident that their story of the world is the story of the world. Everyone is so sure of themselves but what is this based on? Do we analyse the thousands of religious beliefs and choose the one most suitable for us? Or if a religious belief is even suitable at all? Or is our religious belief just the one we learnt about through our family and culture – the first piece of plausible information we received?

This thought experiment relates to religion but we see the same themes with most aspects of our lives and culture. Everyone has their own view of the truth, which is invariably different to most others, who also have their own view of the truth.

When it comes to preferences and tastes, opinions are great, we should all have them. However, when it comes to subjects grounded in science we should learn to construct and defend an argument based on the facts. Unfortunately, we don't learn to do this. We attend regimented schools where we learn to robotically do as we're told but not think for ourselves. By the time we grow up we're so provably ignorant that we lack the capacity to objectively assess the validity of our opinions. Additionally, our opinions have become defining features of our personal identity which further hinders our ability to recognise when they've become indefensible. By the time we reach adulthood most of us no longer want the truth, we just want constant re-assurance that what we believe is the truth[164].

The ignorance pervading our society today is counter-productive to healthy and effective communication between people and leads to a divisive and inharmonious society. This doesn't need to propagate into the future though. Our ignorance needn't be so widespread. Our social system proliferates it by encouraging an overwhelming focus on ourselves to the detriment of understanding the big picture.

3.7. How has money shaped us?

As a result of our cultural immersion in the Monetary System, certain behaviours are encouraged more than others. This influences the way

Modern Religions, page 1 Kenneth Shouler - 2010
163 http://www.gordonconwell.edu/resources/Center-for-the-Study-of-Global-Christianity.cfm
164 http://www.sciencedaily.com/articles/c/confirmation_bias.htm

most people behave most of the time:

- Self-interested: With scarce resources there is an overwhelming focus on self-interest
- Afraid: With people out for themselves we live in a state of perpetual fear
- Greedy: With not enough for everyone we chase limitless money which compromises our character
- Materialistic: With ownership essential for survival we end up valuing material things more than people
- Robotic: With disciplined workers needed we learn to follow procedures rather than think for ourselves
- Ignorant: With such an insular perspective we fail to understand the way our world works

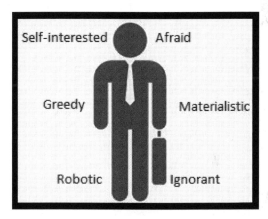

These are some of the traits naturally encouraged and rewarded as a result of the structure of our social system. They're negative behavioural outcomes we experience far too much of in the Monetary System. If we want to change these underlying habits of our behaviour and promote other more positive ones then we need to change the cultural environment that conditions our behaviour. We'll investigate this further in Chapters 6-9.

4. WHAT SITUATIONS HAVE EMERGED IN OUR SOCIETY?

4.1. Introduction

When our social system has things like competition, inequality, and scarcity inbuilt, people are encouraged to behave in a selfish, robotic, greedy, and materialistic manner. When we have that type of social system which encourages those types of behaviour, situations emerge that reflect that circumstance.

Many of us today feel empowered. We feel like we can direct our own future. This feeling of empowerment is a façade though. Rather than being empowered, we're enslaved. We're not enslaved to any evil people though. We're enslaved to the inhumane social system we unwittingly created for ourselves.

In this chapter we'll consider some of the prominent facades that exist today and the contradictory realities that underlie them.

4.2. Voting

Façade that exists

Voting allows us to have our say regarding the future of our country. Our choices help to shape our future.

Reality we face

Voting is our chance to have our say but do we actually know what we're voting for?

Research

This study asks voters to name a political policy they feel strongly about. Then they're asked to explain the detailed mechanics of the policy and the merits of their position vs other positions. Making people explain the mechanisms of policies forced them to confront their own ignorance. The majority of participants failed to account for the complexity of the policy in question, leading to votes that were often misrepresentative of their own values and preferences.[165]

It's simple enough to conduct this research on ourselves. Think about your own country. For each major political party, describe the mechanics of their position on say Education, Environmental policy, and Foreign policy. How did you go? Chances are, not very well. These things are all critical for the functioning of your country though. If you don't have an intimate knowledge of these things, should you really be voting?

In the unlikely event you understood not just the policies above, but every policy for every party, we must then ask the next question. What happens when you support one party's policies on say, Justice, Housing, and Labour, but another party's policies on say, Immigration, Health, and Defense? In that case, we're stuck. We can't vote on each policy. We can only vote for a leader.

This isn't our fault though. Political policies are a convoluted mess of sleep-inducing information. How can we know enough about all policies to make an informed decision to vote when:

1. We're so busy working we simply don't have enough time to consider all the relevant policy information
2. Policy information is presented to us in a dry and boring manner, resulting in general voter malaise

Consequently, most of us place our votes based on a few newspaper or television sound-bites of the leader of the political party. Unfortunately, these sound-bites are getting shorter. The average sound-bite by a U.S presidential candidate in 1968 was 42.3 seconds. Two decades later, it was 9.8 seconds. Today, it's just a touch over seven seconds and well on its way to being supplanted by 140-character Twitter bursts.[166,167] As a result of this, our political opinions (and consequently our votes) are based on very little substantive information. This is how people like Donald Trump get elected into power.

4.3. Politicians

---

165 http://pss.sagepub.com/content/24/6/939
166 http://onlinelibrary.wiley.com/doi/10.1111/j.1460-2466.1992.tb00775.x/abstract
167 http://www.macleans.ca/politics/america-dumbs-down/

Façade that exists

Politicians make decisions in the best interests of the country and its people.

Reality we face

As the following study proves, politicians make decisions in the best interests of the wealthy, not the best interests of most people.

Research

This study tracked 1,800 U.S policy changes between 1981 and 2002 and compared the outcome with the expressed preferences of median-income Americans, the affluent, business interests, and powerful lobbies. They concluded that average citizens "have little or no independent influence" on policy in the U.S, while the rich elite routinely get their way. "The majority does not rule". Rather, politicians exist as puppets for the wealthy.[168]

This research relates to U.S politics specifically but we see the same basic problems in politics worldwide[169,170]. Democracy (society governed by all citizens equally) quantifiably does not exist. What exists is Plutocracy (society governed by the wealthiest citizens). Why are so many of us unaware of these legislations which benefit the rich but harm the average citizen? Because the boring manner in which legislation is presented allows it to be passed through for the elite without the burden of public participation.

It might seem like politicians are being painted as evil people. They're not though. Politicians are just human beings running the same biological hardware as the rest of us (a brain). Like us, they've grown up in a world of things like self-interest and competition. Unlike us though, they've acquired unimaginable levels of power (which we know is physiologically intoxicating even in small doses). Furthermore, they're immersed in an environment of proven institutionalised corruption on a day-to-day basis. Knowing how the human being fits into their environment like one cog wheel into another, we can begin to understand why most politicians are

---

168 https://scholar.princeton.edu/sites/default/files/mgilens/files/gilens_and_page_2014_-testing_theories_of_american_politics.doc.pdf
169http://www.eods.eu/library/NDI.Money%20in%20Politics.%20A%20Study%20Of%20Party%20Financing%20Practices%20In%2022%20Countries.pdf
170 http://www.cnn.com/2012/01/24/world/global-campaign-finance/

the way they are (seemingly dishonest pigs but actually just human beings ticking along in tune with the clockwork of nature). Even if we elected people with the highest moral character, they wouldn't go unaffected in the face of such formidable power and omnipresent systemic corruption.

4.4. War

Façade that exists

Wars occur when groups of people disagree on something. War is an unfortunate but unavoidable consequence of human beings having different views and opinions.

Reality we face

War is complex and has many influences and causes. However, a common theme underlying most wars throughout history - either as the primary cause or a contributing factor – has been a scarcity of resources[171,172,173]. Scarcity leads to inequality and cultivates a hierarchical structure of greed and power. This is a recipe for perpetual war. When scarcity is built in to our social system, war is also built in to our social system.

War is a tool to provide a better life for the nation who starts it (a nation can be a tribe, religion, country or any group of people with common characteristics). Sometimes the approach is transparent: the aggressor nation conquers another nation and assumes control of their resources. Other times it's more subtle: the aggressor nation rids another nation of their problems (e.g. an oppressive regime or shortage of resources) and promotes their own ideology. This is particularly effective when you have a pyramid scheme ideology like capitalism, whereby the more players that join the game, the better it is for the early adopters.

Pillaging others for selfish reasons is a hard sell for governments today though. With the internet and social media shining a spotlight on our individual thoughts and values, we've developed a stronger moral fibre in our public personas. Consequently, subtle approaches to war have become more common. War in the 21st century is dressed up as a noble

171 http://www.ossrea.net/index.php?option=com_content&view=article&id=264
172 http://ibis.geog.ubc.ca/~lebillon/documents/ecowar.pdf
173 Westing, A.H. (1986). Global resources and international conflict: environmental factors in strategy policy and action. Oxford: Oxford University Press.

crusade. In reality it's the same as it's been throughout history: A way for one group of people to gain control over another group of people, resulting in more resources and a better life for themselves, whether directly or indirectly.

Who starts wars? Do poor nations wage war against wealthy ones? Not often. Typically, the rich go to war against the poor. The poor struggle to mount a decent challenge so for the most part they don't bother. A few frustrated citizens might try to rally a few others but their efforts rarely amount to much. This retaliation by the besieged poor is known today as terrorism. Terrorism is a way to describe disenfranchised poor people protesting the injustices they've suffered at the hands of the wealthy.

Case study
We're told the U.S waged a war in Iraq against terrorism. When we look at the statistics though, we see terrorism didn't really exist in Iraq before the U.S arrived. Only since the U.S occupation has Iraq become a hotbed for terrorism. Poverty and oppression give birth to terrorism.

While the word terrorism has only been popularised in the last couple of decades, the concept of a struggling collective fighting back against a dominant one dates back much further. 40,000 years ago - as the last remaining Neanderthals fought back against the spectre of Homo Sapien dominance – it's not hard to imagine that if the Homo Sapiens had a marketing strategy as effective as the U.S government today, those fledgling Neanderthals may have been known as "terrorists". It's certainly an effective way to stir an emotional fortitude and solidarity among your own people.

When we have a world with inbuilt scarcity, inequality, and greed, we have a world ripe for war.

4.5. Laws

Façade that exists
To maintain order in society we create laws which help us distinguish right from wrong.

Reality we face
The fundamental function of a law is to prevent an unwanted behaviour. Specifically, it prevents behaviours naturally encouraged but not wanted

in a given social system. This means the more laws that exist, the more ineffective the social system is. Today the number of laws continue to grow. There is now no official count of the active laws in existence. The number is too big. While we don't know the total count, in the U.S since 1973 alone there have been 287,851 bills put up for legislation, from which 11,608 new laws have been enacted[174].

For the most part, we all know the difference between right and wrong[175]. Laws don't help us distinguish right from wrong, rather, they help the rich get richer while the poor get poorer. More laws and rules tend to be counter-productive. While the idealistic notion is that more laws are making things fairer, we see that more laws are quantifiably making things more unfair. Laws are supposed to prevent crime but they tend to cause more crime (through the proliferation of inequality).

4.6. Crime

Façade that exists

Criminals are bad people who deserve to be punished for the decisions they make.

Reality we face

On a staggeringly disproportionate level, it's the poor people both actually committing crimes and also being convicted of crimes (often wrongly)[176,177,178]. Growing up poor significantly increases the likelihood of engaging in criminal behaviour later in life [179,180,181,182,183]. But whose fault

174 https://www.govtrack.us/congress/bills/statistics
175 http://www.sciencedaily.com/releases/2015/06/150625112010.htm
176 http://www.publiceye.org/defendingjustice/pdfs/factsheets/11-Fact%20Sheet%20-%20Poverty.pdf
177 USDOJ, Bureau of Justice Statistics, 1995. Survey of State Prison Inmates, 1991. http://www.ojp.usdoj.gov/bjs/pub/ascii/sospi91.txt (May 24, 2005)
178 http://www.law.umich.edu/special/exoneration/Pages/about.aspx
179 Yoshikawa, H. 1994, 'Prevention as Cumulative Protection: Effects of early family support and education on chronic delinquency and its risks', Psychological Bulletin, vol. 115, pp. 28-54.
180 Vold, G.B. & Bernard, T.J. 1986, Theoretical Criminology, Oxford University Press, Oxford, p. 37.
181 Brennan, P.A. Mednick, S.A. & Volavka, J. 1995, 'Biomedical Factors in Crime', in Crime , eds J.Q. Wilson and J. Petersilia, ICS Press, San Francisco, pp. 65-90.
182 Loeber, R. & Stouthamer-Loeber, M. 1986, 'Family Factors as Correlates and Predictors of Juvenile Conduct Problems and Delinquency', in Crime and Justice: An Annual Review of Research, vol. 7, eds M. Tonry & N. Morris, The University of Chicago Press, Chicago, pp. 29-149
183 http://www.bocsar.nsw.gov.au/agdbasev7wr/bocsar/documents/pdf/cjb54.pdf

is it if we grow up in a poor family? The parents? Well no, the parents were also children at one stage, they too are products of the environment they grew up in.

We don't dictate our own behaviour in a silo. It manifests from our symbiotic relationship with everything around us. So when someone commits a crime we should be asking about the set of circumstances this person experienced that compelled them to commit that crime. But we don't. Growing up in the Monetary System we're all taught to look within ourselves for the solutions to our problems. We ask: What could I have done better? What could I have done differently? Where did I go wrong?

4.7. Justice

Façade that exists

The justice system determines innocence from guilt. Those adjudged guilty are bad people. They're sent to prison to be rehabilitated.

Reality we face

The justice system is ineffective at determining the truth because:

- Eye witness testimony is considered the highest form of evidence, despite repeated studies showing it to be the least accurate form of evidence available[184,185]. Most false convictions originally relied on eye witness testimonies that were later shown to be false[186,187]. These range from honest mistakes, to coercion, to misconduct by authorities.[188]
- A good lawyer is more important than a true story[189,190]. To have a good lawyer you need money. A lawyer isn't interested in

184 http://www.psychologicalscience.org/index.php/news/police-photo-lineups-challenged-after-series-of-wrongful-convictions.html
185 Wells, Gary L; Memon, Amina & Penrod, Steven D. "Eyewitness Evidence: Improving Its Probative Value". Psychological Science In the Public Interest, Vol. 7, 2006. 48
186 Scheck, B., Neufeld, P., & Dwyer, J. (2000). Actual Innocence. New York: Random House
187 http://www.innocenceproject.org/
188 http://usnews.nbcnews.com/_news/2012/05/21/11756575-researchers-more-than-2000-false-convictions-in-past-23-years?lite
189 Herzing, Rachel. 2005. "What is the Prison Industrial Complex?" See <http://www.defendingjustice.org>
190 U.S. Department of Justice, BJS, 2000. "Defense Counsel in Criminal Cases" See <http://www.ojp.usdoj.gov/bjs/pub/ascii/dccc.txt> (June 16, 2004).

determining innocence from guilt though, they're interested in defending their client.

Studies show the individual adjudged guilty is often the one with the least money rather than the one who is actually guilty[191,192]. Once adjudged guilty, what happens next? The person is deprived from participation in society. They're locked in an empty room for a period of time. On a grossly disproportionate level, those in prison come from poor families[193,194]. They either:

1. Actually committed a crime as they couldn't afford the things they need to survive
2. Didn't commit a crime but couldn't afford a good enough lawyer

Quote
David Eagleman – Neuroscientist
"Prison is provably criminogenic, which means putting more people in prison causes more crime. Estimates now suggest that 30% of the prison population has mental illness. Prison has become a de facto mental healthcare system, but it isn't the right place for our mentally ill"

4.8. Health

Façade that exists

We all have equal opportunity to be healthy.

Reality we face

As your social class decreases, so too does your health and your chances of being affected by any number of health related issues[195,196]. This is known as the health socio-economic gradient. It plays out a number of

---

191 USDOJ, Bureau of Justice Statistics, 1995. Survey of State Prison Inmates, 1991.
http://www.ojp.usdoj.gov/bjs/pub/ascii/sospi91.txt (May
24, 2005)
192 http://www.law.umich.edu/special/exoneration/Pages/about.aspx
193 USDOJ, Bureau of Justice Statistics, 1995. Survey of State Prison Inmates, 1991.
http://www.ojp.usdoj.gov/bjs/pub/ascii/sospi91.txt (May
24, 2005).
194 http://www.publiceye.org/defendingjustice/pdfs/factsheets/11-Fact%20Sheet%20-%20Poverty.pdf
195 http://ije.oxfordjournals.org/content/30/4/899.extract
196 http://www.uic.edu/classes/osci/osci590/12_1%20The%20Socioeconomic%20Gradient.htm

ways:

- Poorer people have limited access to healthcare and their physical health suffers as a result[197]
- Poorer people have more significant psychological self-doubt and stress, driving further ill-health[198,199,200,201]
- Poorer people - as a result of the limitation and deprivation in their lives - turn to debilitating vices far more frequently such and drinking and smoking as a means to escape from their reality[202,203]

Unfortunately, being poor is not a choice:

- Being poor is something that – for the most part - we're born into
- Once poor it's very difficult for us to consciously steer ourselves into a position of wealth

Today we have an absurd situation whereby money is more important than anything, including our health. The system fails because it identifies us as monetary commodities rather than living beings with health needs.

4.9. Summary

Rules, Laws, Regulations, Politicians, Businessmen, or Celebrities are not responsible for any of the situations we face. The situations are all organic by-products of the structure of our social system. To summarise:

- Voting – Is so complex and boring we don't know what we're voting for
- Politicians – Serve the interests of the wealthy ahead of the interests of society
- War – Is an inevitable consequence of scarcity and self-interest
- Laws – Create further inequality, division, and crime
- Crime – Is committed by poor people rather than bad people

197 http://www.stanford.edu/group/scspi/_media/pdf/Reference%20Media/Adler_1994_Health.pdf
198 http://news.uga.edu/releases/article/uga-research-uncovers-cost-of-resiliency-in-kids/
199 http://www.ncbi.nlm.nih.gov/pubmed/23427259
200 http://pediatrics.aappublications.org/content/129/1/e232.full
201 http://www.theatlantic.com/health/archive/2015/10/how-stress-makes-you-sick/412699/
202 http://www.news-medical.net/news/20130730/Children-who-grow-up-in-poverty-are-more-likely-to-smoke-cigarettes.aspx
203 http://www.sciencemag.org/content/341/6149/976.abstract

- Justice – Does not get served when we focus on punishment ahead of understanding
- Health – Is a privilege enjoyed by the wealthy

5. IS THIS THE BEST WE CAN DO?

5.1. Introduction

In this chapter we'll look at current technology and see if there's opportunities for us to use it to identify a better social system than the Monetary System.

5.2. What is technology?

Technology is all our tools, machines, utensils, weapons, instruments, housing, clothing, communicating and transporting devices, and the skills we use to produce them[204].

Quote
Peter Joseph – Activist
"We can think of technology as a helpful extension of our senses. It's a pencil that allows one to solidify ideas on paper for communication, an automobile that allows one to travel faster than feet would allow, a pair of eye glasses that enable sight for those who need it. Technology reduces human effort, freeing humans from a particular chore or job and improving quality of life"

We humans have been around for over 100,000 years and for 99% of that time our life expectancy has been pretty static. However, just in the last 200 years our life expectancy has almost doubled (in the year 1800 human life expectancy was only 37 years of age, today it's 67)[205,206]. We haven't evolved biologically in that short time but we have evolved technologically, on an exponential scale. Technology is the tool that's largely responsible for improving our lives[207].

When we think of technology we think of the computer in our house, the phone in our pocket, the car in our driveway, and the TV in our lounge.

---

204 Read Bain, "Technology and State Government, "American Sociological Review 2 (December 1937): 860.
205 https://www.cia.gov/library/publications/the-world-factbook/rankorder/2102rank.html
206 https://www.youtube.com/watch?v=1ulzS1uCOcE
207 http://www.thezeitgeistmovement.com/

The technology we use is often faulty so many of us see it as unreliable. When it comes to the technology most of us can afford, this is a fair assessment. However, the technology most of us can afford doesn't reflect our technological capability as a species.

What do we mean by technological capability? We mean the technology we have the collective resources and knowledge to produce, regardless of whether we can individually afford it. Our actual capabilities are decades ahead of the technology being used today. Why is that?

5.3. Why can't we utilise our actual technological capability?

For a technological discovery to make it into our day-to-day lives it must be economically viable. For something to be economically viable the cost to produce it must not be greater than the income received from it.

Case study

Economic viability is the reason humans still work in manufacturing jobs. We developed the capability for robots to work on production lines in the 1960's. That technology could free us of this work so why wasn't it rolled out immediately? In the Monetary System, new technological capabilities are not a shared resource for all to use. New technologies are the intellectual property of the person or organisation that created them. They set the price to maximise profit for themselves. As a result, the cost of buying robots to replace humans has remained prohibitive for decades. It's not economically viable. It's cheaper to continue employing humans.

Over time the cost has come down and the number of humans working on production lines is decreasing. But for the majority of the world the use of robots in manufacturing is still not economically viable, even after more than 50 years. This is a perpetual problem with all new technological capabilities. Money is the barrier to utilising our technological capability - not resources, knowledge, ability, or ingenuity. Just money.

5.4. What is our actual technological capability?

This section is focused on understanding our current technological capability as humans – stuff we have the resources and knowledge to make regardless of whether we can afford to. An entire book could be written on our technological capabilities but we'll just focus on some that have the potential to significantly improve our lives.

Energy

The UN estimates by 2030 we'll need 50% more energy than we do today[208]. Do we have the technological capability to produce the energy we need?

- **Solar** - Based on a conservative estimate of current efficiency of solar energy cells (20%) and sunlight hours (70%), we could produce enough energy for the entire world using solar power on an area only $1/18^{th}$ the size of the Sahara desert[209]. That's with today's capability, although it's noted that every year since 1975 the efficiency of solar cells has been improving and is likely to continue to do so[210,211]. Not only is solar continually becoming more efficient, it's also becoming easier to maintain, with the latest solar plants 100% self-cleaning[212]. With current solar power capabilities alone we could power the entire world today.
- **Wind** – Much like solar, we could power the world entirely with current wind capabilities using an area a fraction the size of the Sahara desert[213].
- **Other renewable energy sources** – While solar or wind individually could supply the world's energy needs, there's also other technologies with tremendous potential:
  - o Latest wave power technology can harness 90% of a waves' energy, making it 64 times more effective per square metre than solar power[214].
  - o Biofuels are a broad energy producing capability but one recent development enables crude oil to be created from algae within minutes in the lab. This process takes millions of years in nature[215].
  - o Geothermal power could also supply the world's energy needs but today the cost is prohibitive[216,217].

---

208 http://www.syngenta.com/global/corporate/sitecollectiondocuments/pdf/publications/our_indus try_2012_en_low_res_mail.pdf
209 http://landartgenerator.org/blagi/archives/127/comment-page-1
210 http://www.gizmag.com/artificial-graphene/30845/
211 http://www.nrel.gov/ncpv/images/efficiency_chart.jpg
212 http://www.gizmag.com/ecoppia-e4-ketura-sun/31428/
213 http://landartgenerator.org/blagi/wp-content/uploads/2009/08/AreaRequiredWindOnly.jpg
214 http://newscenter.berkeley.edu/2014/01/28/seafloor-carpet-catches-waves-to-harness-energy/
215 http://www.sciencedaily.com/releases/2013/12/131218100141.htm
216 Cothran, Helen (2002), Energy Alternatives, Greenhaven Press, ISBN 0737709049
217 Fridleifsson, Ingvar B (2001), "Geothermal energy for the benefit of the people", Renewable and Sustainable Energy Reviews 5 (3): 299, doi:10.1016/S1364-0321(01)00002-8

Our population is growing and so is the proportion of people using energy consuming technologies. That doesn't necessarily mean we need more energy though because we're also developing more energy efficient capabilities.

We can convert rainwater to electricity[218], generate fuel from artificial leaves on trees[219], convert garbage to fuel[220,221], convert plastic to fuel[222], convert seawater to fuel[223], convert food waste to natural gas[224], convert human excrement to power buses[225], build roads that harvest energy from the sun[226], power lights using gravity[227], create wires with supercapacitance that double as batteries[228], create electricity from walking with a backpack[229], power supermarkets solely from their food waste[230], create electricity from windows[231], and create light from bleach-filled water bottles[232]. We've built a 15 story apartment block powered exclusively by algae embedded in the walls[233] and built many concept houses that produce more energy than they consume. One of them heats, cools, and powers the home and then also powers the car and gives some energy back to the grid[234].

Water

We have a shortage of water: There are 800 million people without access to safe drinking water[235]. The UN estimates by 2030 the world will need 30% more water than it did in 2012[236]. Further to this, a recent study

218 http://www.gizmag.com/pluvia-rainwater-microturbine/31379/
219 http://newsoffice.mit.edu/2011/artificial-leaf-0930
220 http://www.avfallsverige.se/fileadmin/uploads/forbranning_eng.pdf
221 http://www.edmonton.ca/for_residents/garbage_recycling/biofuels-facility.aspx
222 http://www.plastic2oil.com/site/home gizmag.com/pilot
223 http://www.navy.mil/submit/display.asp?story_id=80171
224 http://www. -organic-waste-biogas-plant/21407/
225 http://www.geneco.uk.com/About-Us/News.aspx?ID=14
226 http://www.solarroadways.com/intro.shtml
227 http://gravitylight.org/
228 http://today.ucf.edu/new-nanotech-may-provide-power-storage-cables-clothes/
229 http://www.gokinpacks.com/
230 http://www.fastcoexist.com/3033413/this-sainsburys-supermarket-is-powered-completely-by-food-waste-which-it-has-a-lot-of
231 http://gravitylight.org/
232 https://www.youtube.com/watch?v=o-Fpsw_yYPg#t=123
233 http://phys.org/news/2013-04-algae-powered-hamburg.html
234 http://www.gizmag.com/honda-smart-home-energy-producing/31380/
235http://www.worldometers.info/?utm_expid=49399924.0Y_Tg2BdRXO9JttgTgd4aA.0&utm_referrer=https%3A%2F%2Fwww.google.co.nz%2F
236http://www.syngenta.com/global/corporate/sitecollectiondocuments/pdf/publications/our_industry_2012_en_low_res_mail.pdf

suggests our current approach to food and water production globally is ill-equipped to deal with our growing population and will lead to widespread civil uprising and a breakdown in social order within the next 30 years[237].

Do we have the technological capability today to address this food and water shortage and avoid a global catastrophe? First, let's focus on water technologies:

- A new pump bottle will make any water sterile in a matter of seconds. You fill it up from the sea (or any muddy pond, river or lake), put the lid on, pump a handle a few times and clean drinking water comes out[238].
- One of the most abundant sources of fresh water is in the air. The Earth's atmosphere contains 4,000 cubic miles of water at any one time[239]. Water-from-air technologies are now relatively common with over 50 companies developing them[240]. Basic technologies can already extract up to 5,000 litres of drinkable water per day from the air[241]. Smaller models the size of microwaves can produce up to 20 litres per day. Some of these run on solar power so they don't require energy from the grid[242].
- The ocean is our most abundant source of water. We have the technological capability to desalinise water from the oceans, making it clean and drinkable. We can also use solar power to desalinise water, making it completely renewable and leading to an endless clean water supply[243,244].
- About 95% of all water that enters most people's homes goes back down the drain in one shot[245]. Even without the latest technologies we could eliminate the shortage just by improving process efficiency.

---

237 http://www.lloyds.com/~/media/files/news%20and%20insight/risk%20insight/2015/food%20system%20shock/food%20system%20shock_june%202015.pdf
238 https://www.youtube.com/watch?v=rXepkIWPhFQ
239 http://www.gizmag.com/extracting-water-from-the-air/2796/
240 http://www.smithsonianmag.com/innovation/this-tower-pulls-drinking-water-out-of-thin-air-180950399/?no-ist
241 http://www.gizmag.com/extracting-water-from-the-air/2796/
242 http://phys.org/news163415064.html
243 http://www.iflscience.com/technology/scientists-develop-thirsty-nanopore-water-filtration-device
244 http://www.newscientist.com/article/mg21028075.400-hot-solar-cells-are-the-cool-way-to-water-and-power.html
245 Use Less-Save More, Jon Clift & Amanda Cuthbert, 2007

Food

We currently have a shortage of food: We have 900 million people undernourished (1 in 8 humans)[246]. 11% of the Earth's land is currently being used for crop production (a big strain on arable land) and we still have so many undernourished[247]. Do we have the technological capability today to address this?

- We've created vertical farms - effectively a skyscraper purpose-built to grow food. A 30 story vertical farm on a 7 acre plot can feed 50,000 people per year today, although the efficiency and output of vertical farms is improving dramatically each year[248,249]. With vertical farms we could achieve the same level of production we do today using only 0.02% of the Earth's land instead of the current 11%[250]. Put another way, if all land currently used for traditional crop farming was replaced with vertical farms we could feed 3.7 trillion people (590 times the current population)[251]. Vertical farms can be built where they're needed and be managed by farmers using a smartphone app. This means only a fraction of the manpower is required compared with traditional farming methods.
- We can also engineer trees to grow multiple types of fruits – one is now growing 40 different types of fruit[252]. Just a few of these trees in every street could provide an endless and varied supply of fruit for the entire world.
- We can grow meat in a laboratory using tissue samples from muscle cells of animals. One tissue sample can create up to 20,000 tonnes of meat[253].

---

246 http://www.worldometers.info/?utm_expid=49399924.0Y_Tg2BdRXO9JttgTgd4aA.0&utm_referrer=https%3A%2F%2Fwww.google.co.nz%2F
247 http://www.fao.org/docrep/005/y4252e/y4252e06.htm
248 http://gogreen.whatitcosts.com/vertical-farm.htm
249 http://www.newscientist.com/article/mg22129524.100-vertical-farms-sprouting-all-over-the-world.html?full=true#bx295241B1
250 assumes 7 acre, 30 storey vertical farm can feed 50,000 – then, total land area on Earth is 5.4 billion acres, total population is 7.2 billion. 7.2 billion people divided by 30,000 people = 144,000 vertical farms needed. 144,000 multiplied by 7 acres = 1 million acres needed, out of total land area of 5.4 billion acres = 0.02% of Earths land area needed.
251 11% currently used is 550 times the 0.02% needed. 550 multiplied by 6.3 billion currently well nourished = 3.7 trillion people able to be fed
252 http://www.treeof40fruit.com/
253 http://www.gizmag.com/cultured-beef/28584/

- Over 30% of all food produced in the world is wasted[254]. Even without the latest technologies we could eliminate hunger simply by reducing waste. We've already developed concept kitchens to do just that[255].

Production and Manufacturing

Robotics – Robots are used in manufacturing, assembly, packing and packaging, transport, Earth and space exploration, surgery, weaponry, laboratory research, safety, customer service, farming, building, and the mass production of consumer and industrial goods[256,257,258,259,260]. We have robots that can hop[261], fly[262], skate[263], climb[264], swim[265] and sail[266]. We also have robots that can build other robots[267], jump on top of buildings[268], run faster than humans[269], learn from talking to humans[270], read and respond to human emotions[271], and look almost exactly like humans[272]. They can work together and complete tasks without duplicating effort[273], teach themselves to work without having any prior knowledge of their form or function[274], adapt to injuries and continue working[275], and they have their own internet where they can standardise, learn from other robots, and share knowledge[276]. We've started teaching robots to understand

254 http://www.bbc.co.uk/news/world-europe-13364178
255 http://www.conceptkitchen2025.com/
256 Robotics: About the Exhibition". The Tech Museum of Innovation
257 http://www.miraikan.jst.go.jp/en/exhibition/future/robot/android.html
258 http://sydney.edu.au/news/84.html?newscategoryid=2&newsstoryid=13686
259 http://icd.uni-stuttgart.de/?p=11173
260 http://serva-ts.com/product.2.0.html
261 http://www.ai.mit.edu/projects/leglab/robots/3D_hopper/3D_hopper.html
262 Testing the Limits". Boeing. p. page 29.
263 Commercialized Quadruped Walking Vehicle "TITAN VII"". Hirose Fukushima Robotics Lab.
264http://www.intechopen.com/books/international_journal_of_advanced_robotic_systems/capuchin-a-free-climbing-robot
265 Robotic fish powered by Gumstix PC and PIC". Human Centred Robotics Group at Essex University. Retrieved 2007-10-25
266 Jaulin, L.; Le Bars, F. (2012). "An interval approach for stability analysis; Application to sailboat robotics". IEEE Transaction on Robotics 27
267 http://www.sipixdigital.com/foambot_robot.html
268 http://www.bostondynamics.com/robot_sandflea.html
269 http://www.bostondynamics.com/robot_cheetah.html
270 http://tellmedave.cs.cornell.edu/
271 http://www.softbank.jp/en/corp/group/sbm/news/press/2014/20140605_01/
272 http://www.geminoid.jp/en/robots.html
273 http://www.dtic.mil/dtic/tr/fulltext/u2/a479478.pdf
274 http://www.sciencedaily.com/videos/401217.htm
275 http://www.iflscience.com/technology/robots-can-adapt-injury-within-minutes
276 http://roboEarth.org/

morality and ethics[277] and one robot has flown to space[278]. With current capabilities, robots can perform almost any task a human can and in most cases they can do it better.

3d printers - A 3d printer takes a digital design from a computer and uses that to print a real 3d object. The first 3d printer was invented and successfully printed a real object in 1983[279]. Since then they've been used to manufacture anything from prosthetic limbs, to furniture, to pizza for astronauts in space, to parts of a military jet plane, to an entire car, to an unmanned flying drone, to clothing, to part of a human skull, and even human tissue[280,281,282,283,284]. The latest 3d printers are capable of building an entire multi-level house in less than 24 hours, including all plumbing, electrics, windows, and cladding[285,286]. Alternatively, they can build 10 basic single-story houses in one day[287]. In a combination of 3d printing and robotics, 3d printing robots can now work together to autonomously build large scale structures[288]

3d printers can also print themselves, meaning once you have one, you effectively have as many as you want[289]. 3d printers can be used to manufacture anything within the bounds of human imagination. You effectively draw an object on a computer using a 3d printing program then hit print. If you aren't that imaginative, you can also download specs of any item you want to manufacture, then hit print.

Nanotechnology – Nanotechnology is the manipulation of matter on an atomic or molecular level, generally defined as being between 1-100

277 http://www.gizmag.com/machine-ethics-artificial-intelligence/32036/
278 https://twitter.com/AstroRobonaut
279 http://www.3dsystems.com/30-years-innovation
280 http://www.baesystems.com/article/BAES_164442/3d-printed-metal-part-flown-for-first-time-on-uk-fighter-jet
281 http://www.gizmag.com/bioprinting-human-tissue-harvard/30928/
282 http://www.ibtimes.com/3d-print-color-stratasys-reveals-objet500-connex3-worlds-first-multicolor-multi-material-3d-printer
283 http://beta.slashdot.org/story/198397
284 http://www.medicaldaily.com/3d-printed-polymer-skull-implant-used-first-time-us-244583
285 http://www.businessinsider.com.au/3d-printer-builds-house-in-24-hours-2014-1
286 http://rt.com/usa/3d-printed-concrete-house-727/
287 https://www.youtube.com/watch?v=OYqBxEAtXZA
288 http://iaac.net/printingrobots/#robots
289 http://www.gizmag.com/tour-aleph-objects-lulzbot-factory-hq/31024/

nanometres[290,291]. One nanometre is one billionth of a metre, meaning the comparative size of a nanometre to a metre is the same as that of a marble to the size of the Earth[292]. The first manipulation of atoms using nanotechnology occurred in 1989 yet it remains very much in its infancy today. Nanotechnology has already been used to create new super materials such as artificial Graphene and Buckypaper, which have limitless applications in building, space, and aeronautics[293]. Buckypaper for example is 1/10th the weight and hundreds of times stronger than steel[294].

In a combination of nanotechnology and robotics, DNA Nanobots have successfully been injected into cockroaches, found their way around, folded and unfolded DNA, and delivered necessary drugs to affected cells[295].

We have the capability today to produce an abundance of resources for all people, whether it be energy, food, water, shelter, transport, goods, or services. Unfortunately, it isn't economically viable to utilise our latest capabilities and improve our lives. Money is preventing us from improving our lives.

5.5. What drives these new technologies?

Quote
Buckminster Fuller – Designer, Inventor, Author
"Humanity is acquiring all the right technology for all the wrong reasons"

We have some amazing technological capabilities but is it the best we could have done? More than half the U.S Research & Development budget goes to Defense (wars, weaponry, and military technology). The U.S spends more money developing new technology for Defense than it spends on Health, Energy, Agriculture, Transportation, Space, Science, and

290 Drexler, K. Eric (1986). Engines of Creation: The Coming Era of Nanotechnology. Doubleday. ISBN 0-385-19973-2.
291 Drexler, K. Eric (1992). Nanosystems: Molecular Machinery, Manufacturing, and Computatin. New York: John Wiley & Sons. ISBN 0-471-57547-X
292 Kahn, Jennifer (2006). "Nanotechnology". National Geographic 2006 (June): 98–119
293 http://www.gizmag.com/artificial-graphene/30845/
294 Future planes, cars may be made of `buckypaper'". Yahoo! Tech News. 2008-10-17. Retrieved 2008-10-18.
295 http://www.newscientist.com/article/dn25376-dna-nanobots-deliver-drugs-in-living-cockroaches.html

Education combined[296]. A huge amount of the technology we're developing each day is designed to kill other human beings, whether it be directly or indirectly.

Advancing our lives under the guise of death and destruction is a dangerous foundation on which to build a society. What kind of species dedicates so much of its intellectual resources to killing each other, especially when so many still live in conditions of abject poverty or lack the basic necessities of life.

Case study

In the 1940's the U.S Government created the Manhattan Project – used to develop the atomic bomb. This project employed 130,000 people. Imagine if those engineers, chemists, physicists, and technicians had been working on medical or technological advancements that could improve our lives rather than blow people up.[297]

We're nowhere near as advanced as we could be because our social system pre-occupies us with selfishly scrambling for resources to help build a better life for our own country at the expense of those in other countries.

5.6. Is technology making our lives easier?

We lead very busy lives today. We frantically rush around with barely enough time to stop and think. Life in the early 21st century wasn't supposed to be so hectic though.

In the 1950's, economists predicted that by 1990, Americans would work 22 hours a week, six months a year, and retire before age 40[298]. They sure did have rose tinted glasses back then. Maybe those 1950's economists acquired some early samples of the drugs that would come to define the 60's. In any case, the average worker is now on the job about one month longer per year than they were in the 50's[299]. We're also retiring much later. Why is that?

It's because in the Monetary System we need to work, in order to earn

296 http://www.thenewatlantis.com/publications/the-sources-and-uses-of-us-science-funding
297 http://en.wikipedia.org/wiki/Manhattan_Project
298 http://www.stuff.co.nz/life-style/life/9861533/Are-busier-people-happier-really
299 http://www.scu.edu/ethics/publications/iie/v8n1/timetogohome.html

money, in order to survive. We're so deep in this cultural rabbit hole that we've lost sight of what we actually want. What do we want? Is it a job? No, we just want access to what a job gives us. And what's that? Is it money? No, we just want access to what money gives us. And what's that? It's energy, food, water, shelter, goods, and services that we can use for our survival, entertainment, enjoyment, and stimulation - enabling a safe, happy, and fulfilled life. That is what we actually want.

Unfortunately, it's becoming increasingly difficult for us to afford the things we actually want[300]. Our lives haven't been made easier, despite having the technological capability to do so. We're not working less, despite having the technological capability to do so. In the Monetary System, technology can never make our lives easier by freeing us of the need to work because we need to work, in order to earn money, in order to survive.

5.7. Can technology save our planet?

There's a popular narrative that we can all have anything we want if we just work hard for it. Unfortunately - as long as we're in the Monetary System – that's an impossibility.

Case study
If everyone were living the lifestyle of the middle class in the U.S, the Earth would be able to sustain 2 billion people (the current population is over 7 billion). Americans consume roughly 3.3 times the subsistence level of food and about 250 times the subsistence level of clean water[301]. Even if all 7 billion people worked their asses off (which most people already are), there would still only be enough stuff for 2 billion people to have the lifestyle of middle class Americans[302].

While the Earth is indeed overpopulated in the context of the Monetary System, it is not overpopulated per se. There is enough land area in the state of Texas alone for every human being on the planet to live comfortably. This assumes an individual having a 100sqm unit or an average family having a 400sqm house and yard. In other words, there is

---

300 http://stateofworkingamerica.org/charts/productivity-and-real-median-family-income-growth-1947-2009/
301 http://mmcconeghy.com/students/supcarryingcapacity.html
302 http://www.worldwildlife.org/pages/living-planet-report-2014?amp&amp

enough space for 212 times the current population to live comfortably.[303,304]

Furthermore, we know we have the technological capability to produce enough energy, food, water, goods, and services for many multiples of the current population. The problem we face today is not over-population, it's inefficient and wasteful consumption – an inherent part of our social system[305].

If we utilise our technological capability we can manage our resources sustainably and abundantly, enabling a high quality of life for every human being on the planet. Unfortunately we have a social system that won't allow it. Our social system ensures money is prioritised ahead of resources and technology. An almost unfathomably stupid situation.

5.8. Money is a disenabler

We have the technological capability for every single human being on the planet to have a high quality of life. Despite having this capability there are still:[306,307,308,309,310,311,312]

- 900 million people undernourished
- 800 million people without access to clean drinking water
- 2.5 billion people without a toilet
- 1.2 billion people without access to electricity
- 1 billion people living in inadequate housing
- 100 million people homeless
- 40 million people displaced from their homes due to civil unrest
- 27 million people being exploited in illegal slavery
- 34,000 children dying every day from poverty and preventable diseases

303 http://data.worldbank.org/indicator/AG.LND.TOTL.K2
304 https://overpopulationisamyth.com/overpopulation-the-making-of-a-myth
305 http://valhallamovement.com/blog/2014/11/08/overpopulation-fact-myth/
306 http://www.worldometers.info/?utm_expid=4939992-
12.aYZmajl9QlGwBb2_cpXNaw.0&utm_referrer=https%3A%2F%2Fwww.google.co.nz%2F
307http://portal.unesco.org/shs/en/files/4363/10980840881Pogge_29_August.pdf/Pogge+29+August.pdf
308 http://www.un.org/en/globalissues/briefingpapers/food/vitalstats.shtml
309 http://www.washingtonpost.com/blogs/wonkblog/wp/2013/05/29/heres-
310 http://www.un.org/cyberschoolbus/habitat/units/un05hous.asp
311 http://www.homelessworldcup.org/content/homelessness-statistics
312 http://books.google.ca/books/about/Disposable_People.html?id=YqTwql3SZbgC&redir_esc=y

- 40% of the population living on less than $2 a day
- More than half of all people without access to the internet
- Everyone without access to the latest technology, instead getting technology that will inevitably break

Today we hand over money and in return we get electricity, housing, clothing, food, and water, so we naturally perceive money as something that enables us to get the things we need. In reality money doesn't enable these things at all, rather, it:

- Disenables new technology
- Disenables the preservation of resources
- Disenables an equal and fair world
- Disenables a happy, civilised society
- Disenables creativity and freedom
- Disenables the solving of problems due to the requirement for profit
- Disenables an abundance of resources for everyone due to the requirement for scarcity

Money is a disenabler. Money is a significant barrier to progress and a significant threat to our future existence. It's survived recessions, depressions, inequality, wars, famines, genocides, and more, all without the system ever really being questioned. In the last few millenia we've questioned almost everything about our existence, except money.

Case study

The library of Alexandria was one of the most significant libraries of the ancient world. It flourished for almost three centuries during a great knowledge revolution. It was a time when science came of age and we questioned almost everything. During that time the world's foremost scholars and scientists were in Alexandria re-defining our understanding of so much of the world around us – from the size of the Earth, to the position of the stars, to the basis of geometry, to the composition of our anatomy, to the function of medicine, to the first concepts of things like steam engines and robots. Despite almost everything about our existence being questioned, there's no record of anyone ever seriously challenging a single political or economic assumption of the society in which they lived. Money, and its inherent structures, were never questioned.[313]

---

313 https://en.wikipedia.org/wiki/Library_of_Alexandria

While this example focuses on Alexandria, the same hesitance to question the Monetary System has been apparent throughout the past few thousand years of human society and remains today. Money has been the most unquestioned form of faith in our history. Throughout the world we speak 7,000 different languages, obey several hundred different rulers, and worship over 4,000 different gods, yet we all believe in money created through fractional reserve banking – the process used in every country in the world today.

In light of the discoveries we've made about money, it's hard to imagine an intellectually respectable position from which to defend it. Nevertheless, some of you may be thinking it's still appropriate, and if so, that's probably because it's working for you, because you are doing well in the Monetary System. However, just because the system is working for you, does not mean the system is working.

Quote

Jiddu Krishnamurti – Philosopher, Author, Speaker
"It is no measure of health to be well adjusted to a profoundly sick society"

5.9. The wrong questions

The wrong questions are being asked. Instead of asking "how much will it cost?" we should be asking "do we have the resources?". With our technological capability today we can design a world where the question of "how much will it cost?" becomes redundant. Why do we keep asking what it costs? What does that even mean?

Monetary costs are really just a figment of our imagination. They're completely detached from our technological capability and planets resources. Money is essentially some pieces of imaginary paper we use to place value on resources. It's a shackle, enslaving us into a hypnotic state of social paralysis.

In times of recession we ask "how much does it cost?", and the answer is usually "too much". This means lots of people don't have access to food, water, and shelter – the basic necessities of life. Is there a shortage of food, water, and shelter? No, there's a shortage of money, a shortage of imaginary paper. This shortage makes people suffer. It's backward - having the amount of money determine how much resources you have is letting the hypothetical tail wag the dog. Resources exist plentifully if we apply our technological capabilities to manage them sustainably.

5.10. Is it time to change our social system?

Quote

Henry Ford – Founder of the Ford Motor Company
"It is well enough that the people of the nation do not understand our monetary system, for if they did, I believe there would be a revolution before tomorrow morning"

We need to re-think the monetary paradigm - and everything that comes with it - and ask ourselves, "Is it necessary? Or could we design something better?"

The way societies are organised determines what they'll be like. For example, consider a society organised on a basis of love and co-operation. Put a hypothetical 10,000 people in this society and they'll naturally care about each other, share things, treat each other with respect, and work together.

Now take another hypothetical 10,000 people and put them in a society organised on a basis of fear and competition rather than love and co-operation. Give those people the same resources and what do you have? You have hoarding, division, belligerence, and a "what's in it for me" mentality[314]. People pull apart and start battling with each other. Many sub-groups form to protect their own patch of resources. In the end a few of these groups gain enormous power and everyone else ends up providing for them.

If you hadn't realised, one of those is the basis of our society today – a world of scarcity, competition, and consequently, fear. We're living in that world already and it doesn't work. We know that now. We need to design a new social system that makes the world better for all of us together, and as a consequence, actually make each of our own lives better, individually.

Quote

Michael Jeffreys – Motivational Speaker

------

314 https://www.youtube.com/watch?v=wwk-Mlm5I24

"The old ways aren't working anymore - the egoic structures, putting people as commodities, as something expendable. The ends don't justify the means. We've experienced lack and limitation enough. We know what it's like to compete with each other, to fight, to say 'I can't give you any of mine because there will be less for me'. We've played that game. It's time to play a new game"

6. COULD WE DESIGN A BETTER SOCIETY FOR OURSELVES?

6.1. Introduction

This book has two main objectives:

1. *To raise awareness of the reality of the Monetary System*: The first step in solving any problem is recognising there is one. Hopefully we now recognise there is a problem.
2. *To raise awareness that a better alternative exists*: The next four chapters will be an exercise in imagining an alternative to the Monetary System. We'll focus on one alternative system. We're not specifically promoting that system though. Instead, we're raising awareness we can do much better than the Monetary System.

We'll consider the core structure of the alternative system (Chapter 6), how we could transition to it (Chapter 7), the ways it'd shape the human experience (Chapter 8), and the situations that might emerge (Chapter 9). Along the way we'll contrast the alternative system with the comparable aspect of the Monetary System (from Chapters 2, 3, and 4).

Before we start, let's think about the prospect of a world without money. Imagine a world that doesn't use money at all – no banks, cash, wages, or bills. No money of any kind. What do we see? Many of us imagine everyone going back to a more primitive lifestyle, living a meagre existence, growing our own crops and livestock like peasants. Or maybe we see a complete breakdown in society – no laws or social order, with those too lazy to grow their own food stealing it from others or maybe even killing each other to survive.[315]

Most of us have this natural assumption of a world without money being a world without order – a world of chaos. Money doesn't create order at all though, rather, it creates disorder. We've seen this pernicious paradox comprehensively demonstrated throughout the first five chapters.

---

315 https://www.youtube.com/watch?v=EyrB4MuMtY0

Without money we can create a far more civilised society than would ever be possible with money.

6.2. Designing our new social system

Before we can design a more civilised society we need to know why our society is the way it is today. What's driving it? Why do we have the Monetary System? Let's recap what we've covered so far:

1. We were faced with a problem that needed solving. That problem was a scarcity of resources.
2. The question we asked was "Who gets what, and why?".
3. This question led to the creation of money to decide who gets what.
4. The creation of money brought about the concept of interest.
5. Interest led to the requirement for more money to continually be created (growth).
6. The requirement for growth has polluted the human experience on an incalculable scale. It's stretching our planets resources, approaching a point of no return, and threatening our future existence.

A sensible progression of events led to where we are today. We identified problems and created solutions. The solutions were logical at the time. They were a response to the key problem we faced throughout history: a scarcity of resources.

Today we have technological capabilities that could enable an abundance of resources. This means we have a new problem to solve. Instead of asking "how do we allocate the scarce resources among the people?" (who gets what, and why?), the question we have the technological capability to be asking instead is "how do we allocate the abundant resources to all the people?"

What do we mean by abundant resources? We mean a plentiful supply of all our needs and wants. That means access to all the energy, food, water, shelter, goods, and services that we can use for our survival, entertainment, enjoyment, and stimulation - enabling a safe, happy, and fulfilled life. Money is an astonishingly primitive tool for a species capable of abundance.

Why would we want to allocate the abundant resources to all the people instead of the scarce resources to some of the people? To make a better world for all of us collectively. With this in mind, we can create a society with a more worthy goal. Rather than a goal of growth, we can strive for "The well-being of ourselves and our planet"

We include the planet in our goal because our well-being is inextricably tied to the well-being of our planet (we cannot survive without our planets resources). To achieve this goal we seek to produce a sustainable abundance of resources. This renders money (a medium of exchange) pointless. We're not looking to exchange resources, we're looking to make them abundant. To make resources abundant it doesn't make sense to live in a society based on money (a Monetary System), it makes sense to live in a society based on resources (a Resource Based System).

6.3. What is a Resource Based System?

Where the Monetary System requires scarcity to enable growth, a Resource Based System requires abundance to enable well-being. In a Resource Based System (also known as a Resource Based Economy), all goods and services are available without the use of money, barter, credit, debt, or servitude of any kind[316]. A Resource Based System utilises the efficiency of technology to provide a sustainable abundance of resources for all.

This concept is not entirely new. Its roots trace back as far as Ancient Greece, although the first concepts closely resembling a modern Resource Based System surfaced in 1833 from a man named John Etzler[317]. Many have advanced and evolved similar concepts in the decades since such as Karl Marx, Thorstein Veblen, and Buckminster Fuller (apparently this concept attracts the eccentrically named)[318,319,320]. Most recently Jacque Fresco and Peter Joseph have refined it and addressed earlier challenges around design, form, and function of the system[321].

How do we allocate the abundant resources to all the people?

316 http://www.thevenusproject.com/about/resource-based-economy
317 The Paradise within the Reach of all Men, without Labor, by Powers of Nature and Machinery: An Address to all intelligent men, in two parts (1833)
318 http://www.technocracy.org/about-us/
319 Howard, E (1902), Garden Cities of To-morrow (2nd ed.), London: S. Sonnenschein & Co, pp. 2–7
320 http://en.wikipedia.org/wiki/Buckminster_Fuller
321 http://www.thevenusproject.com/

How do we get the right item in the right quantity at the right time to the right place? We use modern logistics. Logistics is the process of planning, implementing, and controlling the effective and efficient flow of goods and services from the point of origin to the point of consumption[322]. We can think of it as the application of science to the production and distribution of resources. We use it to determine what needs to be produced, how much needs to be produced, where it should be produced, how it should be distributed, how much should be distributed, where it should be distributed, and to whom it should be distributed.

The logistical system needs to synthesise all information as people are born, people die, people move, preferences change, resources are used, new technology is developed, and new processes are created. All of these things are constantly changing and the system must dynamically update to ensure a sustainable abundance of resources for all. Do we have this sort of logistical capability today?

Logistical computers, methodologies, systems, and management are already widely used by almost every large corporation in the world today. The same approach that puts food on our tables and phones in our pockets today would be followed. We'd just be working together to do it more efficiently rather than working for ourselves to do it more profitably.

Achieving an abundance of resources is not something we could achieve overnight though. A Resource Based System – and all the components of that system – could only be realised with a gradual transition. We'll explore the transition in more detail in the next chapter.

6.4. The consequences of the social system

In Chapter 2 we saw how the core structure of a social system influences everything. Money – in its inherent structure:

1. Requires a continuous and never-ending growth in the money supply
2. Which can only be achieved amidst conditions of relative scarcity

The inherent requirement for growth implies necessary scarcity. This cascades down to shape everything else.

---

322 http://cscmp.org/sites/default/files/user_uploads/resources/downloads/glossary-2013.pdf

A Resource Based System, in its inherent structure:

1. Requires our well-being, rather than growth
2. Which can only be achieved in conditions of abundance, rather than scarcity

The inherent requirement for well-being implies necessary abundance. This cascades down to shape everything else.

The paradigm difference between the two systems seems almost counterintuitive at first. However, it doesn't take much examination to appreciate the paradoxical dichotomy. This will become increasingly clear over the next four chapters. First, let's recap the consequences of the Monetary System:

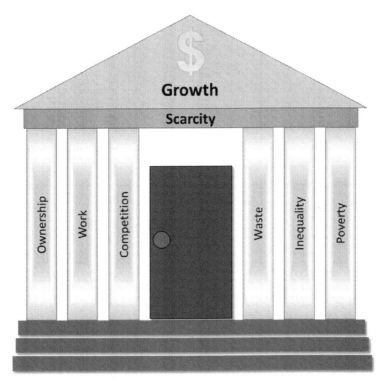

Now we'll take a closer look at a Resource Based System. We'll explore the consequences of this social system compared with our current one. We'll start with the first pillar – ownership.

6.5. Access, not ownership

In our current social system, private ownership is widespread and deep-seated, precisely because it better enables us to charge money for things. Today almost everything is owned by someone, making things seemingly scarce. Ownership helps to preserve the artificial scarcity the Monetary System requires[323].

For some things (e.g. sentimental items or things we use often) ownership is culturally important and makes sense. However, many things we enjoy today are impersonal low-usage items. For these low-usage goods it's inefficient, unsustainable, and impractical for us to own one each. Imagine everyone having their own holiday home, boat, jet-ski, sports car collection, private jet, and so on. Those who own these things use them only a few times per year and the rest of the time they sit unutilised. Individual ownership of all goods is illogical to aspire to. It consigns most of us to a life of limitation unnecessarily.

While it's impossible for everyone to own one of everything, that doesn't mean we couldn't all have access to one of everything. We could. We have the technological capability to achieve a very high level of production and manufacturing that could provide an *access abundance*. An access abundance means we produce enough so that – based on average expected usage at any one time – everything is in plentiful supply. It means each of us can access far more than we do today, whether it be boats, snowboards, cars, holiday houses, cinemas, musical instruments, restaurants, golf courses, or anything we so choose. We could all access more than we could dream of individually owning. If we all have access to everything, ownership becomes largely irrelevant.

While we'd need to increase production of some things (which we have the technological capability and resources to do), many other things are already in plentiful supply. They're just largely unutilised due to the inefficiency of ownership.

Case study
In the U.S there's around 12 million vacant homes at any one time.

---

323 Hume [1739] 1888, pp. 484–98

Meanwhile, 600,000 people are homeless[324,325,326]. That's more than 20 vacant homes for each homeless person. A plentiful supply already.

Case study

In the U.S there's 88 million adults interested in recreational boating. There are 12 million boats. The average boatie spends 9 days per year on their boat. If we assume 3 adults per voyage, the average boat is used 22 days per year only. This leaves 333 days with boats sitting unutilised.[327]

Isn't ownership part of human nature?

For 99% of our species time on Earth, we shared, we co-operated, we didn't have money, and we didn't conceive of private ownership[328,329]. Biologically speaking we're pretty much the same as our ancestors who existed without private ownership. Only extremely recently (in evolutionary terms) have we developed agriculture, and with it, a sense of ownership of the land we settled[330,331]. Ownership is not built into human nature, it's built into the Monetary System.

Nevertheless, it's a deep-seated cultural value within us all and a transition away wouldn't be easy. It'd need careful management and gradual phasing, probably on an inter-generational scale (we'll cover this in Chapter 7). In some ways this transition is already under way though, with many things being shared today that never were in the past:

We share holiday homes and even our own homes (think Airbnb), cars (RelayRides and Getaround), rides in our own cars (Zimride, SideCar and Lyft), music (Spotify), movies (Netflix), boats (timeshare ownership is common), bikes (Spinlister), internet (Fon), goods with others in our community (Neighbour Goods), many of us now live with others (house-sharing is increasingly common), and we're even starting to share less tangible assets such as time, space, skills and money (TaskRabbit, Zaarly

324 https://www.hudexchange.info/resources/documents/ahar-2013-part1.pdf
325 http://www.census.gov/programs-surveys/ahs/
326 http://usatoday30.usatoday.com/money/economy/housing/2009-05-14-govtown_N.htm
327 http://www.statista.com/topics/1138/recreational-boating/
328 Waldron, Jeremy (1988), *The Right to Private Property*, Oxford: Clarendon Press
329 http://provokateur.com/wp-content/uploads/2012/01/The-Pale-Blue-Dot.pdf
330 http://www.context.org/iclib/ic08/gilman1/
331 http://www.henrygeorge.org/pchp29.htm

and Lending Club).[332,333,334,335,336,337,338,339,340,341,342,343]

Younger generations are coming to the sobering realisation that spending $30,000 on a car that sits parked and unutilised for 23 hours a day is wasteful and inefficient. Over the past decade we've seen car ownership among millennials dropping dramatically while car sharing services like ZipCar are booming.[344]

Quote
Tom Goodwin – Author
"In 2015, Uber – the world's largest taxi company, owns no vehicles, Facebook – the world's most popular social media, creates no content, Alibaba – the world's most valuable retailer, has no inventory, Airbnb – the world's largest accommodation provider, owns no real estate"

A sharing and access-focused culture is not only consistent with human nature, it actually improves our nature. We'll explore this more in Chapter 8.

6.6. Automation, not work

Today we work because we need to work, in order to earn money, in order to survive:

1. As society advances, the work naturally becomes more specialised and robotic
2. We have to work to survive but we don't enjoy being forced to do a robotic job
3. We don't enjoy it because we're motivated by self-direction, not by following procedures

---

332 http://neighborgoods.net/
333 https://www.taskrabbit.com/how-it-works
334 https://www.spinlister.com/
335 https://www.netflix.com/ca/
336 https://www.lyft.com/
337 https://www.airbnb.com
338 https://zaarly.com/
339 https://www.lendingclub.com/
340 https://zimride.com/
341 https://relayrides.com/
342 https://www.getaround.com/
343 https://corp.fon.com/en
344 http://www.theatlantic.com/magazine/archive/2012/09/the-cheapest-generation/309060/

4. So to prepare us for the boring specialised work we've been moulded into robots growing up

Today this all makes sense. Robotic work is a necessary evil to enable our high standard of living. However, without a system which requires us to work an incredible opportunity presents itself: Instead of grooming our children like robots to do the required robotic jobs, we can design robots to do the jobs for us, freeing us of the need to work.

This doesn't mean we'll have 7 billion R2D2's rolling around though. We're not talking about robots as you might imagine them from Hollywood movies. We're talking about the automation of the jobs required in the production and distribution of resources. We're talking about a world designed for technological automation. Things wouldn't be designed to be operated by humans, nor would they be designed for robots that look like humans. Rather, they'd be designed for mechanisation and automation.

Case study
A supermarket designed for automation wouldn't need robots walking around stocking shelves. It could be designed so driverless trucks unload the food and it conveys automatically to the shelves where we grab the food. With no money there would be no checkouts, it would all be free. The technology to create an automated supermarket and supply chain like this exists today. Of course, we'd still need to carefully manage the transition.

The mechanisation and automation of labour

Mechanisation is the process of doing work with machinery[345]. For thousands of years - from the agricultural revolution, to the invention of the plough, to the industrial revolution, to the invention of the steam engine – we've built things that make our lives easier. However, only in the last few centuries have we advanced from mechanisation to automation[346].

We're probably all aware of the early types of automation in factories producing things like shoes, clothes, computers, cars, sports equipment,

---

345 Willis, Robert (1861). Principles of Mechanism: Designed For The Use Of Students In The Universities And For Engineering Students Generally
346 http://www.britannica.com/EBchecked/topic/201583/fantail

and musical equipment. Additionally, in Chapter 5 we covered automated solar power plants, automated vertical farms, and 3d printing robots that build houses. But there are plenty more examples of automation today we might not be aware of:

We have fully automated restaurants[347], automated garbage collection[348], automated mining, including automated trucks and railways to deliver mined minerals to their destination[349], automated fruit picking[350], automated tractors[351], automated dairy farms[352], automated laboratories[353], robot-run hotels[354], robots that inspect products other robots have built[355], robot nurses[356], robot pharmacists[357], robots in retail customer service[358], robot librarians, call centres, secretaries, and travel agents[359,360], robot surgeons that outperform human surgeons[361], robot cleaners that memorise the layout of property, vacuum the house, mow the lawns, and clean the pool[362], robots that cook any meal you want then clean up and wash the dishes[363], robot police officers[364], robot guides in museums[365], robot bartenders[366], and robots that work in vineyards[367].

Our automated technologies are much better than us at following the

---

347 http://www.foxnews.com/story/2009/08/06/robot-chefs-run-restaurant-in-japan/
348 http://www.kcrg.com/news/local/Automated-Garbage-Trucks-Hitting-Cedar-Rapids-Streets-181070351.html
349 http://sourceable.net/rio-tinto-launches-automated-mine-future/
350 http://www.gizmag.com/artificial-vision-orange-sorting/20184/
351 http://www.gizmag.com/automated-self-steering-tractor/19883/
352 http://www.stuff.co.nz/business/farming/dairy/10610178/22m-robotic-dairy-shed-among-worlds-biggest
353 http://www.technologynetworks.com/lims/
354 http://www.smithsonianmag.com/travel/japan-announces-plans-first-hotel-run-robots-180954168/?no-ist
355 Graves, Mark & Bruce G. Batchelor (2003). Machine Vision for the Inspection of Natural Products. Springer. p. 5. ISBN 978-1-85233-525-0.
356 http://cs.stanford.edu/people/eroberts/cs181/projects/2010-11/ComputersMakingDecisions/robotic-nurses/index.html
357 http://www.ucsf.edu/news/2011/03/9510/new-ucsf-robotic-pharmacy-aims-improve-patient-safety
358 http://www.nzherald.co.nz/business/news/article.cfm?c_id=3&objectid=11349679
359 http://bigstory.ap.org/article/practically-human-can-smart-machines-do-your-job-2
360 http://www.technologyreview.com/featuredstory/515926/how-technology-is-destroying-jobs/
361 https://www.sciencedaily.com/releases/2016/05/160504151855.htm
362 http://www.telegraph.co.uk/technology/news/11074345/Dyson-unveils-intelligent-robot-vacuum-cleaner.html
363 http://www.iflscience.com/technology/robot-chef-home-could-arrive-2017
364 http://www.robots.com/articles/viewing/police-robots
365 http://www.lincoln.ac.uk/news/2014/05/896.asp
366 http://monsieur.co/#about
367 http://agmechtronix.com/Products/AVP/

specialised, robotic tasks required for the production and distribution of our resources. They don't need breaks, don't sleep, don't take holidays, and don't make anywhere near as many mistakes.

If you give a man a fish he eats for a day. If you teach a man to fish he eats for life. What if you build a robot to fish though? If you build robots to work in a Resource Based System, we all eat for life. If you build robots to work in the Monetary System, a tiny few get very rich and the rest of us starve. As sure as the sun will rise tomorrow, robots will continue to be built to work. We can't prevent our robotic capabilities improving but we can change the social system in which we manage them.

How much can we automate?

Keep in mind, we don't need to replace all jobs that exist today. We only need to replace those that contribute to the production and distribution of resources. Any job relating to money would no longer exist. And how many jobs is that?

In the U.S, the industries of financial, business, professional, and government services account for one in every three jobs[368]. Add to that any sales, accounts, payroll, administration, finance, business, marketing, advertising, or management function from other industries. Straight away almost all of these would be eliminated as they're irrelevant in a world without money.

The majority of today's jobs contribute nothing to producing the goods and services we need for our survival, enjoyment, stimulation, and fulfilment. The majority of today's jobs are fictitious manifestations of a society based on some pieces of imaginary paper. They would be socially pointless in a Resource Based System. Most other jobs we have the technological capability today to at least partially (and in many cases fully) automate[369,370,371].

Quote
Peter Diamandis – Physician

368 Employment Projections Program, U.S. Department of Labor, U.S. Bureau of Labor Statistics
369 http://www.amazon.com/Race-Against-Machine-Accelerating-Productivity/dp/0984725113/ref=sr_1_1?s=books&ie=UTF8&qid=1397641254&sr=1-1&keywords=Race+Against+The+Machine
370 http://www.amazon.com/The-End-Work-Decline-Post-Market/dp/0874778247
371http://www.mckinsey.com/insights/business_technology/four_fundamentals_of_workplace_automation

"I can imagine a day in the future where the patient walks into the hospital and the patient needs, say, cardiac surgery, and the conversation goes something like this: 'No, no, no, I do not want that human touching me. I want the robot that's done it 1,000 times perfectly"

Full unemployment

Today every country blindly strives for full employment. Full employment is the unquestioned goal nobody stops to think twice about. In our current social system it makes complete sense (because we need to work to earn money to survive).

In a Resource Based System - without money - we wouldn't have this constraint. Driven by the well-being of ourselves and our planet – we'd strive for full *unemployment*, rather than full employment.

Working hard can be extremely rewarding but only if we're working hard at something worth doing. A robotic job that could be automated is absolutely not worth doing for any human. Success in a Resource Based System would not be based on getting a job to earn money to survive. Instead, it'd be based on discovering individual passions and pursuing those. We'd spend our time doing things that make our lives enjoyable, fulfilling, stimulating, and worth living. More on the mechanics of this in the next chapter.

Of course, actually achieving *full* unemployment may never be possible but even with today's technology it's estimated we could be working only one day per week[372]. However, with projected improvements in technology over the coming decades this should reduce dramatically.

Before we move on, let's address some concerns that may have cropped up.

Concern: If people didn't have to work they'd become lazy and do nothing

We know we're not motivated by working at a job, but rather, we're motivated by choosing to do something that matters to us and getting better at that. We wouldn't sit around getting fat and lazy. That's what we do today and we do that because we're spending our lives forced to do

---

372 http://issues.org/30-3/stuart/

jobs we don't enjoy.

Research

In this study, everyone within a community was delivered a minimum wage to live off. It was enough so they could do nothing if they wanted. Instead of doing nothing, productivity went up, education attendance went up, more kids graduated than ever before, doctor and hospital visits went down due to the decreased stress from having financial security, people became proud of their community which they felt a part of together, and as a result people were pitching in to help one another and giving back to the community.[373]

This study – and others like it[374,375,376,377,378] - demonstrate when our basic needs are provided for without needing to work, we don't become fat and lazy. Instead, we become happier and more productive.

Research

A massive meta-analysis of 128 studies was conducted into the effect of money on our motivations. Money was shown to decrease motivation for activities where there was previously a non-monetary motivation. This applies to anyone doing something they're passionate about - such as scientists, inventors, explorers, musicians, advanced technologists, and artists – the type of people who make our lives more enjoyable and drive progress forward. These people don't do what they do for money and studies show when they get paid for it they enjoy it less. People do these things because they're passionate about them, not because they get paid for them. Without a requirement to work its likely many more of us would engage in productive pursuits.[379]

Concern: I don't want a world run by robots with no human interaction

A mature Resource Based System wouldn't be a world without human

---

373 http://www.dominionpaper.ca/articles/4100
374 http://economics.mit.edu/files/10849
375http://www.guystanding.com/files/documents/Basic_Income_Pilots_in_India_note_for_inaugural.pdf
376 http://papers.ssrn.com/sol3/papers.cfm?abstract_id=2268552
377 http://papers.ssrn.com/sol3/papers.cfm?abstract_id=2439488
378 http://www.nber.org/papers/w21340
379http://www.rug.nl/gmw/psychology/research/onderzoek_summerschool/firststep/content/papers/4.4.pdf

interaction. In fact, it would be the opposite. There wouldn't be anyone slaving over us in service roles but there would be more meaningful human contact in our day-to-day lives than we experience today. How would this happen?

When we have an abundant society with plentiful free time and no divisions based on status or wealth, we're awarded more opportunities to form relationships with far more people than ever before. No hidden agendas, no people serving us and smiling because they're paid to, but more genuine friends than we could ever hope for today. This is one of the most beneficial by-products of a Resource Based System, given scientific studies now repeatedly show that having meaningful social relationships is the single most important factor in making us happy[380,381].

6.7. Co-operation, not competition

In a Resource Based System we'd all have access to an abundance of resources and we wouldn't spend a lifetime working to be able to afford them. Rather, the abundance we enjoy would be free. This can't happen if we continue to compete as we do today though. Competition is not conducive with global abundance and automation. We need to co-operate if we want to achieve these things.

A planetary society

Today we have 198 countries all guarding their own information and resources. This is counter-productive to producing an abundance of resources though. Making resources abundant is not a political problem, it is a logistical problem. Consequently, countries and governments would lose relevance in a Resource Based System (albeit they'd still be needed in the transition).

Many of us haven't really considered a world without countries because they've existed our entire lives – we live in one and so does everybody else. However, it doesn't take too much retrospection to realise the concept of a country is just another turn in the road toward a planetary society.

380 http://www.hup.harvard.edu/catalog.php?isbn=9780674059825
381 http://www.theatlantic.com/business/archive/2016/04/why-so-many-smart-people-arent-happy/479832/

Hundreds of thousands of years ago it was 'us vs them' – our small hunting group vs other small hunting groups. Then tribes arose, it was 'us vs them' – our tribe vs other tribes. Those grew to become villages, towns, cities, and now countries. It's still 'us vs them' though. We're just beginning to dip our toes in the next turn on the road with things like the European Union – a group of countries banding together with a shared monetary currency and inter-governmental co-operation.

All along the road for the past few hundred thousand years, our collectives have been getting bigger. We're developing more friends and less enemies, wider trusted communities. The next step is to overcome the competitive 'us vs them' mentality altogether and adopt a co-operative approach whereby it's just us – humans – and we're all in it together.

Losing countries and governments doesn't mean we lose our diversity or culture though, these would remain. Diversity and culture have countless fruits to bear. We wouldn't want to lose that. However, the idea that our country determines our access to resources, our rules, our laws, our beliefs, our quality of life, and our ability to travel is all inappropriate. It's restrictive and harmful and only relevant in a world of money.

The power of co-operation in accelerating progress

Today competition is widely understood to be a good thing and in a monetary society this is true. Competition ensures profit-driven corporations produce the best products that can realistically be expected for the price. In a monetary society, competition leads to many efficiencies and makes complete sense. This is why capitalism has become the dominant economic system - because capitalism promotes competition and competition breeds efficiency, making capitalism the most efficient economic system within the Monetary System.

However, competition is only the most effective way to make progress within a monetary framework. In a Resource Based System, we would naturally co-operate as it's far more effective in achieving an abundance of resources to improve our well-being.

Case study

Today there are 115 corporations worldwide that manufacture mobile phones. Each has their own technical experts, scientists, engineers, programmers, and developers, all trying to figure out better ways to build the same item. If one of those experts makes a discovery it's kept private. It's their intellectual property used to provide a competitive advantage and increase profit. It may be years before the technical experts from the other 114 mobile phone manufacturers have each individually made the equivalent discovery. In this scenario we have hundreds of scientists, engineers, programmers, and developers, all trying to figure things out that – collectively as a species – we've already figured out.[382]

This is a shameful waste of the talented people advancing our quality of life. Today all information and resources are owned by the person, corporation, or country that discovered them. They use those discoveries to benefit themselves and those who can afford to pay for them.

In a Resource Based System - without ownership or money - the notion of withholding information for private gain becomes irrelevant. Any new discovery or technological capability would naturally be shared with everyone. We'd all collectively benefit from the efforts of everyone else.

Open-sourcing to reduce corruption and increase trust

We wouldn't just co-operate by sharing discoveries, we'd co-operate by making the production and distribution of resources visible to everyone. This is a concept that's already becoming more popular today, it's called open-source. Open-sourcing would be a cornerstone of the system. We'd use it to mitigate against corruption and improve trust. With everything open-sourced it's much harder for an elite group to game the system for their own advantage.

The internet is a key enabler in successfully open-sourcing the day-to-day functioning of a society. The lack of internet (and with it the lack of open-sourcing capability) is a key reason why past efforts at similar social change failed. More on this shortly.

We don't need rules and laws to make this so, just like there are no rules or laws making us compete in the Monetary System. We compete today as a natural consequence of the structure of the social system. Similarly, in an open-sourced Resource Based System, we would co-operate as a natural consequence of the structure of that social system.

---

382 http://en.wikipedia.org/wiki/List_of_mobile_phone_makers_by_country

6.8. Conservation, not waste

Money is inherently wasteful for two key reasons:

1. It encourages inefficient production and consumption of our finite resources
2. It restricts new technologies because they aren't affordable

In a Resource Based System - with no money and a goal of well-being – we could utilise our technological capability to preserve our finite resources and provide a global sustainable abundance. We'd do this by co-operating to improve both our processes and products.

Case study

Building the average American home produces up to 7 tonnes of waste in the process[383]. Furthermore, most of the 220 million tonnes of waste generated each year in the U.S ends up in one of the over 3,500 landfills[384]. As we know, we have the technological capability to build 3d printing robots capable of building entire houses. With this method there is no waste. Furthermore, we know we have the capability to make all houses self-sustaining energy producers. There is nothing stopping us doing this. The only barrier today is money.

Today products break or become outdated quickly, enabling them to be re-purchased in a short period of time and maximise profit. In a Resource Based System – with no requirement for profit - products would be designed differently. All products would be designed:

1. To last
2. To be recycled when they do eventually break
3. To update so parts that are quickly outdated are universally replaceable, updatable, and interchangeable (e.g. computer chips, smart phone hardware)

At an individual level, conserving would be encouraged if our lives depended on the collective sustainability of our social system rather than the individual size of our bank accounts. It'd be clear we couldn't use more than the natural regeneration of the Earth's resources, much like its

---

383 http://www.cardinalgroup.ca/nua/ip/ip01.htm
384 http://center.sustainability.duke.edu/resources/green-facts-consumers/how-much-do-we-waste-daily

clear today we can't spend more than we have in our bank accounts.

6.9. Equality, not poverty and inequality

Inequality and poverty are in-built today because:

1. Resources are inherently scarce, meaning everyone must try and get as much as possible for themselves.
2. Wealth tends to be passed through the generations.

In a Resource Based System – with no money and abundant resources - nobody is competing to get as much as they can for themselves. Poverty and inequality wouldn't exist. Our goal is well-being and we achieve this goal utilising our technological capability to provide an abundance of resources for all. Basic provisions such as food, water, and shelter are things we know we have the capability to produce an abundance of. Of course, it wouldn't just be food, water, and shelter we'd have an abundance of, we'd have an access abundance of everything for everyone. Without money we'd all be rich.

6.10. Summary of a Resource Based System

We're already familiar with the structure of the Monetary System and the ways it influences society. What about a Resource Based System? How would it influence society?

The well-being of ourselves and our planet
Abundance

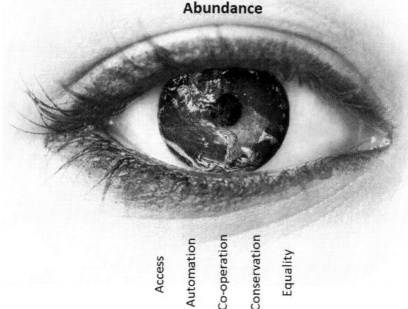

Access · Automation · Co-operation · Conservation · Equality

Whether its socialism, liberalism, capitalism, fascism, or communism (the practical application of it in history to date) - all of these are political ideologies grounded in exchanging resources with a form of money. They all have waste, competition, the drudgery of excessive work, ruling elites, divisive nation states, taxation, scarcity, and of course, money. None of the existing political systems is an abundant, sustainable, planetary society designed for the needs of human beings and the planet that supports us. That's precisely what a Resource Based System is and why it's a polar opposite of the existing systems or ideologies tried in the Monetary System. The existing ideologies are all far closer relatives to one another than a Resource Based System is to any of them.

6.11. Comparison with communism

Communism, in the original sense of the word, is a political ideology theorised by Karl Marx in the 1800's. It has never realistically been attempted. It does have much in common with a Resource Based System though. It has no money, no government, and the utilisation of technology to reduce or remove work, allowing us time to fulfil our passions and express our individuality and creativity.

For most of us today, the word communism has a different meaning. We think of the failed centrally planned economies spearheaded by the Soviet Union throughout the 20th century(These "communist" states were distinctly uncommunist though.) They were oppressive totalitarian regimes claiming to aspire to communism but their devotion to this goal was questionable at best. They were in many ways, truly dreadful social systems. Unfortunately, due to communisms association with those failed systems, it has become a dirty word.

The communism that failed - the one referred to by almost everyone today - is very different to a Resource Based System. The failed states had many dreadful features that have no place in true communism or a Resource Based System[385,386,387,388,389,390]:

- Centrally planned economies with oppressive rules
- No democracy or elected governments
- Culture strictly controlled and regulated by government
- Significant spending dedicated to militarization
- Emigration restrictions
- Secret police enforcing obedience by all
- Press and media run by the state and completely subservient to the state
- Mandated expropriation and nationalisation of private property
- Labour camps for anyone who spoke out against the collective
- Inefficient crony control structures that led to mass famine
- Methods for producing abundance that contradicted the accepted scientific understanding of the time
- No internet, openness, or transparency of processes

---

385 https://www.amazon.com/philosophical-socialism-religion-critique-world-at-large/dp/1176992112/ref=sr_1_1?s=books&ie=UTF8&qid=1495926486&sr=1-1&keywords=9781176992115

386 Hardt, John Pearce; Kaufman, Richard F. (1995), East-Central European Economies in Transition, M.E. Sharpe, ISBN 1-56324-612-0

387 Crampton, R. J. (1997), Eastern Europe in the twentieth century and after, Routledge, ISBN 0-415-16422-2

388 T. B. Bottomore. A Dictionary of Marxist thought. Malden, Massachussetts, USA; Oxford, England, UK; Melbourne, Victoria, Australia; Berlin, Germany: Wiley-Blackwell, 1991. Pp. 54

389 Wettig, Gerhard (2008), Stalin and the Cold War in Europe, Rowman & Littlefield, ISBN 0-7425-5542-9

390 Applebaum, Anne (2003) Gulag: A History. Doubleday. ISBN 0-7679-0056-1

- And of course, money, tax, scarcity, and the drudgery of work

Even if the failed states genuinely wanted to reach communism, they were ill-equipped to achieve it. This will be expanded on in Chapter 7 when we explore the transition.

6.12. Comparison with the Monetary System

Let's compare the basic structure of a Resource Based System to our modern capitalist Monetary System.

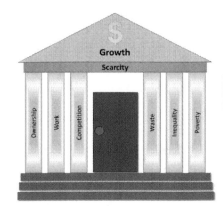

The goal is growth	The goal is well-being
Which requires scarcity	Which requires abundance

- 198 countries
- 100 million corporate agendas
- 180 monetary currencies
- Ownership makes things scarce
- Work is necessary to survive
- Competition is highly inefficient
- Discoveries benefit few
- Technology is constrained
- Waste destroys our planet
- Processes waste resources
- Products break or expire quickly
- Inequality divides us
- Poverty is widespread

- 1 planet
- 1 agenda – our well-being
- No money
- Access provides anything we need
- Automation frees us from labour
- Co-operation lifts productivity
- Discoveries benefit all
- Technology is always utilised
- Sustainability saves our planet
- Processes best utilise resources
- Products last, recycle, or update
- Equality unites us
- Poverty doesn't exist

Growth requires scarcity

What we see here is two systems with paradigm differences in their structures. In one system we suffer and in the other we prosper. It's possible today to create a world we enjoy rather than a world we endure, a world that values life more than it values money.

6.13. How suitable is each system for the needs of a human being?

Now we have a clear picture of the differences between the Monetary System and a Resource Based System, let's score their suitability for human beings. We have the following needs:

Physical well-being:

- Food
- Water
- Shelter

Emotional well-being:

- Safety & security (having the confidence to stretch ourselves)
- Love & belonging (feeling equal, as though we're all in it together)

Motivation:

- Autonomy (our desire to be self-directed)
- Purpose (our desire to do something important, something that matters to us)
- Mastery (our desire to get better at what we do)

How well does each system cater to those needs?

Physical well-being

- 900 million undernourished
- 800 million without clean water

- Nobody undernourished
- Nobody without safe drinking water

- 2.5 billion without a toilet
- 1.2 billion without electricity
- 100 million people homeless

- Nobody without a toilet
- Nobody without electricity
- Nobody without a home

Emotional well-being

- Half of us live on less than $3 a day
- Stratified society with few peers
- With scarce food, water, and shelter it's risky to follow our dreams so we get a safe job that pays the bills

- Everyone has abundant resources
- No divisions based on status or wealth
- With guaranteed food, water, and shelter we can follow our dreams and reach our full potential

Motivation

- 90% of us do not enjoy our jobs
- At work we follow procedures and aren't trusted to think for ourselves
- Mastering a menial and pointless process provides little satisfaction

- We do something that matters to us
- Not required to work, we're free to express our creative talents
- Mastering a creative pursuit that matters is rewarding

A Resource Based System caters to all our needs while the Monetary System caters to none. Money is not evil though, it's just the training wheels we've used for thousands of years in a long epoch of scarcity. With that very important variable (scarcity) being overcome, money has become obsolete[391].

Case study

Even as little as 200 years ago when someone came up with the revolutionary idea that everyone should be entitled to an education funded by tax-payers, most people thought the idea was outrageous. We thought street kids were incapable of learning and it was a waste of money. We thought only rich kids from privileged families were capable of learning. How primitive that seems now? And that was only 200 years ago. Even in the last 200 years we've learnt so much more about ourselves, let alone since the creation of money thousands of years ago.

---

391 http://www.debate.org/opinions/would-it-be-beneficial-to-switch-to-a-resource-based-economy

7. HOW COULD WE TRANSITION TO IT?

7.1. Introduction

We now understand the structure of a Resource Based System and how it differs to the Monetary System. How do we get from A to B though?

In this chapter we'll explore a hypothetical transition to a Resource Based System. We'll assume a cold turkey approach, in other words: We pick a day and after that, money has no value. We wake up the next morning in a developing Resource Based System.

This doesn't mean we wake up in a radically different world though. That wouldn't work. We wouldn't cope with the culture shock of such sudden changes to our way of life. As a result, many would wake up the next morning and go to the same job as they do today. This will become clearer as we progress.

The timings suggested in this chapter are highly speculative. Building a detailed transition plan would be a huge undertaking. We're not doing that here. We just want to visualise a path to a Resource Based System to demonstrate it's far from an insurmountable challenge.

7.2. Preparing for transition day

All the preparation work would be undertaken while still in the Monetary System so it'd need funding from a consortium of governments, institutions, and corporations. The funding would be invested into developing the technology and paying the specialists to carry out the preparation work. What would that work look like?

- Collecting information about people and resources
- Setting up the logistical system
- Determining who gets access until we make things abundant
- Determining the priorities

7.3. Collecting information about people and resources

Collecting information about people

We'd need to conduct a global survey to understand how each person can contribute during the transition (because while we'd strive for full unemployment, in order to build the automated abundance we'd need as many hands on deck as possible). We'd ask questions such as:

- What's your current job?
- What other skills do you have?
- What type of work would you like to do?

A Resource Based System is an empowered social system. This means everyone has the option to work or not. How do we know everyone wouldn't refuse to work? Because the reward for work in the transition is far greater than the reward for work today. The reward is a foreseeable future where work is minimal and we have an abundance of resources. Keep in mind, everyone already has to work hard today. We wouldn't need to do more than that, we'd just get far greater rewards in return (abundance and automation). Furthermore, we could be incentivised to do the jobs most in demand. More on this shortly.

We also need to know how people want to live. We'd ask questions such as:

- What kind of goods and services do you want?
- How often would you like to use them?
- Where would you like to live?

While we're empowering people with freedom of choice, we'd still need rules to navigate the transition (ensuring people do their chosen jobs and don't loot all the free food in supermarkets, for example).

Collecting information about resources

We'd also need to collect information about resources. This would enable something of a global "stock-take":

- Where are existing factories for producing goods?
- Where is the available land for new production facilities?
- What technologies do we have for production and distribution?
- What existing goods owned by corporations could now be shared? (We'd also need to find this out about individuals. More on this shortly).

7.4. Setting up the logistical system

With detailed information about ourselves and our resources, the logistical system could inform us:

- Collectively how to get the right item in the right quantity at the right time to the right place (for example, who does what to help build an automated abundance)
- Individually how to access the goods and services we want (for example, if you want to take a boat out, or see a movie, or book a venue for a party, you need to know how to do that. We could use a simple app)

More on these things shortly.

7.5. Determining who gets access until we make things abundant

We can classify resources in two broad categories - needs and wants. How can we distribute them until we make things abundant?

An approach to distribute the needs

Today we have a massive disparity in the distribution of needs (food, water, housing, infrastructure, and utilities). Consequently, those in poorer countries often want to migrate to richer countries. Too much migration can overload infrastructure though, so this might have to be restricted during the transition. That doesn't mean we couldn't take holidays or migrate to countries with lesser quality of life. We could. We'd just be placing restrictions on *upward* mobility. This is really no different to the situation today. Furthermore, these restrictions would only apply initially, until such time as we achieve an abundance of our basic needs.

An approach to distribute the wants

Today rich people get almost everything regardless of what it means to them, such as tickets to concerts and sports events, the ability to travel to any exotic place, and all the latest toys. The rich have a monopoly on these things even though many buy them just because they can. Meanwhile, people who would give everything for these things simply cannot afford them.

In a Resource Based System – without money or hierarchy - a preference-based approach could determine who gets what. We could load our preferences into an app. The app could inform who wants any given scarce resource most on any given day. For popular things where preference alone couldn't determine who gets access, we could factor in contribution (those who offer to work where needed most have priority over those doing sought after jobs or those not working at all). If we still can't determine priority of access, we could randomly allocate it among those left.

Case study

For example, you might load the following preferences into the app for next Saturday:

1. Go and watch your team play football
2. Take a boat out with friends
3. Spend a night at a holiday home

If the football stadium holds 60,000 and only 55,000 people want to go, you would get a ticket. However, If 100,000 want to go then it would go to the next measure, contribution. If 80,000 of the 100,000 people are contributors (still more than the 60,000 seats the stadium holds) then we could consider the type of contribution they make. We could reward those doing jobs nobody wants to do (like sewer cleaners) by giving them priority over people doing jobs many people want to do (like travel tour guides). If after factoring in contribution we still couldn't determine an appropriate hierarchy to allocate the 60,000 tickets, the remaining tickets would be distributed using the next measure, random allocation.

If you aren't allocated one of the 60,000 tickets, you move to the pool of people wanting your second preference (taking a boat out). The same process is followed until eventually you get to enjoy one of your favoured scarce resources. With this approach we'd have maximum utilisation of scarce resources on any given day.

This approach would ensure far more people get access to far more stuff than they do today. It would enable everyone a realistic opportunity to experience the things most important to them (whether in work or play). Keep in mind, this would only be needed until a given resource is made abundant (or for the occasional things we can never make abundant, such as seats to popular one-off events).

There are many possible approaches to distribute scarce resources without money. This isn't necessarily the best approach, it's just one approach that could facilitate a transition.

7.6. Determining the priorities

A Resource Based System is not a political system so we don't have a bunch of old rich folks throwing round their opinions. Instead, the priorities are logically deduced from our goal (the well-being of ourselves and our planet)

1. **Survival** – The first thing we require for our well-being is an abundance of basic needs.
2. **Enjoyment** - Secondly, we require an abundance of the nice-to-haves (the wants).
3. **Automation** – Thirdly, we automate the production and distribution of these things.
4. **Cultural transformation** – And finally, our values and behaviour gradually transform in response to our new social circumstance.

Of course, we have many hands so all these things would be happening simultaneously. We'd just be prioritising needs ahead of wants and wants ahead of automation. As the transition progresses we'd be working less, having access to more, and becoming better human beings in the process. This is the opposite of the past few decades where we've been working more, having access to less, and struggling to fulfil our potential.

With all this preparation work complete (collecting information, setting up the logistical system, determining who gets access until things are abundant, and determining the priorities) we'd be ready to transition.

7.7. Phase 1: Abundance of needs (first few years after transition day)

In Phase 1 we focus on our top priority – survival. This means producing a sustainable abundance of our basic needs (food, water; housing; infrastructure; and utilities) as quickly as possible. The logistical system could inform the most efficient use of technology, resources, and human labour to do so.

While the initial focus would be basic needs, we'd still want access to everything we currently have (regardless if it's a want or a need).

Nobody's quality of life should decrease (we'd still want to eat Big Mac's, go on holidays, play golf, and drink bottles of wine). With this in mind, if you currently work in the production and distribution of resources (whether it be a need like food production or a want like helicopter tour pilot), you'd probably be incentivised to continue doing that in Phase 1. However, if you currently work in banking, advertising, insurance or any other socially pointless role, you'd now have no job. This represents billions of people available to contribute toward producing an abundance of our basic needs – a lot of hands on deck.

Of course, not everyone wants to build housing and infrastructure and that's perfectly fine. We'd have a shortfall of many other skills (such as solar power technicians, vertical farm managers, and environmental scientists). There'd be a wide variety of jobs in demand. The logistical system could identify the jobs in demand and incentivise us to do them. This would give everyone a realistic opportunity to make a meaningful contribution in a way that stimulates and challenges them personally, but also benefits society collectively.

How long would it take to produce an abundance of our basic needs? This is difficult to forecast because we've never globally co-operated before. We have no comparison. However, we do have historical examples that illustrate how much can be achieved when a group of people are collectively motivated toward a common goal, unhinged from monetary constraints.

Case study
At the beginning of World War II, the U.S had roughly 600 first-class fighting aircraft. They were expensive to produce so the U.S had a limited supply. However, once it became apparent that many more would be needed to win the war, price became less of an issue. Without the typical peace-time economic constraints, the U.S produced 90,000 planes each year during the war, when in all previous years they only managed a fleet of 600.[392]

This illustrates how much production can be increased when unshackled from the usual economic constraints. War-time is the closest we come to understanding our true production potential. Even war-time isn't close to the productivity we could enjoy if completely unshackled from money

---

392 http://www.thevenusproject.com/about/resource-based-economy

with all hands on deck in a Resource Based System though.

For the purposes of this hypothetical transition we'll assume five years to produce a sustainable abundance of life's essentials. This is, of course, very speculative and based on circumstantial rather than direct evidence.

7.8. Phase 2: Abundance of wants (5+ years)

Once everyone has an abundance of basic needs we shift our focus toward producing an abundance of wants (the nice-to-haves). This includes everything from boats, to bikes, to recreational facilities, to movie theatres, to sports equipment, to musical equipment, to electronic and digital devices. We don't need everyone to own one each, we just need everyone to have access when they want it, based on average expected usage. Producing this access abundance of wants would be a two-pronged approach:

1. Sharing existing stuff
2. Producing new stuff

Sharing existing stuff

Everyone would have the option to share their low-usage goods with others. Some would share a lot straight away, others would share nothing. Some will take more time than others to let go of the things they own. It's important nobody is forced to give up anything they own. In an empowered social system it must be on our own terms. During the transition there would be both shared goods and owned goods. This could be managed with something as simple as an app.

Case study
Say you own a trailer. At first you don't want to share it. You don't. After a few months observing other friends sharing their stuff, you decide to share your trailer. You list it on the app as available for sharing. People needing a trailer search for trailers near them. They find yours, they come and use it, then return it.

This approach makes sense for our generation as we seek to minimise radical changes to our way of life. Future generations would probably evolve it to something less rooted in traditional ownership though. The idea of returning things like a trailer would probably lose relevance. Instead they might be used and left at their destination. Next time you wanted a trailer you'd search on the app and find the one closest to you. This type of system could work for many low-usage goods, not just trailers.

With every day that passes, more people would share more of their low-usage goods. Experience suggests this cultural adaptation could happen quickly too (as demonstrated in the obedience study; small scale societies study; power study; and wealth study). Furthermore, studies show when one person behaves generously it inspires others to behave generously later. It can jumpstart a virtuous cycle where one person's generous behaviour can influence many others. It's contagious[393].

Producing new stuff

Sharing alone could enable an abundance in some situations. We have an access abundance of many things already today, we just can't utilise them because of the inefficiency of ownership. However, producing an abundance of all our wants wouldn't happen through sharing alone. There are many things we'd have to increase production of, particularly in poorer countries where resources are scarcer. Fortunately, we have the technological capability to achieve a very high level of production and manufacturing. Furthermore, we'd have many hands on deck helping with that.

How quickly could we achieve an access abundance of wants, through both sharing our existing stuff and producing new stuff? With our readiness to assimilate to new cultural norms and our technological capability to manufacture quickly and efficiently, this could happen fairly quickly. We'll assume an additional five years to cultivate an access abundance of most of our wants. Again, a speculative figure based on circumstantial evidence.

7.9. Phase 3: Automation (10+ years)

Once we can sustainably produce an abundance of needs and wants we'd look to remove the human labour component. Of course, many things would already be automated during Phase 1 and 2 while producing an abundance. In Phase 3 we'd be automating the things not already

---

393 http://www.pnas.org/content/107/12/5334.abstract

automated.

In some cases we'd need to develop new technologies but most jobs can already be automated today (albeit we can't afford to). With every day that passes, the average workload of the average person would decrease until we reach something close to full unemployment. How long this takes is difficult to determine but after a decade of concerted effort it's hard to imagine anyone having to work much more than a day a week.

By this stage we'd have the comfort to follow our dreams, fulfil our passions, and spend our lives doing whatever stimulates and challenges us. At this point the fundamental nature of our nature on an individual and collective level would undergo a more substantial transformation.

7.10. Phase 4: Cultural transformation (20+ years)

The human brain cultivates very different versions of human nature when it exists in very different social circumstances. While a cultural transformation would start from transition day onward, the changes would be more pronounced once we have abundance and automation. When we don't have to compete with others for quality of life, and there's nobody suffering unnecessarily, and our social system collectively provides for everyone, then yes, of course, we will change. However, while our brains re-wire every day, these changes are constrained by the basic neural foundations established during our formative years.

Quote
David Eagleman – Neuroscientist
"In a two year old a typical neuron has more than 15,000 connections. That's almost twice as many connections as found in an adult. What happens in between? We prune back the possibilities that are initially present. We become who we are not because of what grows in our brain but because of what is removed. As we grow, we reduce the number of connections in our brain in favour of focusing on a smaller number of stronger connections. The links you don't use, you lose"

Growing up today we're rewarded for being competitive, materialistic, and greedy, so connections associated with these things strengthen. Conversely, connections associated with being co-operative, compassionate, and humanitarian - which are not so beneficial in today's world - would have been lost. For this reason, those of us alive today wouldn't experience a complete cultural transformation. It's too late for us.

Only when we have people who've grown up in a world of equality, co-operation, automation, and abundance will we have a completely different version of human nature to that which is familiar today. We don't need to biologically evolve to fix the flaws many of us feel are innate. We just need to change the way we programme our brains and we do this by designing different social circumstances to grow up and grow old in.

Assuming we did that, what might this future look like? We'll explore this in the next two chapters. We'll consider the cultural changes in a civilisation of people that have only known a sustainable automated abundance.

7.11. Summary of high-level transition plan

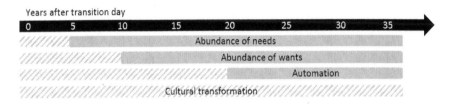

While the timings are speculative and the detail light, we're not trying to answer every little question. We're just trying to imagine a journey to a functioning Resource Based System. We want to understand it's entirely plausible today and worth investigating further to see if we can make it happen. Therein lies our biggest challenge – actually making the decision to transition away from our current social system. This is the challenge we'll address in Chapter 10.

7.12. Past transition failures

Dramatic social change has been attempted before. The attempted transition to communism made by the totalitarian regimes of the 20th century is the most relevant. Where specifically, aside from the many problems noted in Chapter 6, did they fail?

They tried to transition to an empowered social system on a basis of enslavement

In almost all cases throughout the 20th century, the transition was attempted through massive consolidation of power, a totalitarian single party system, and nationalisation and expropriation of private property. The state enslaved the workers with a thinly veiled promise of one day setting them free. The problem here is simple: If you want to transition to a fundamentally empowered social system, you can't do it on the back of oppressive enslavement. Empowerment is critical to the future state so it must embody the transition state.

They tried to transition from a state of social and economic turmoil

The failed states were born out of early 20th century Russia. It was one of the poorest countries in Europe with the majority of its people illiterate, poverty stricken, and working in agriculture. They had just lost World War 1 and endured a five year civil war which hyper inflated the currency and took them to the brink of collapse. This is no foundation for undertaking such a monumental task as transitioning to communism.

They didn't realistically have the ability to produce an abundance

In 1917 when the communist movement began, the technology to produce a sustainable abundance of resources didn't really exist. Technology has improved exponentially in the past 100 years though. We can now produce a sustainable abundance of resources in a transparent, intelligent, and efficient manner. When the failed states took their last breath in 1989, the internet (critical for modern logistics) still didn't really exist in any useful capacity. It was a different world.

They tried to transition to a moneyless world using money

Money has endless leadership hierarchies of privileged individuals and then it has everyone else. This situation is born out of an individualistic and private world where everyone tries to get as much as possible for themselves. Communism, in theory, is a collectivist and open world without money where everyone works for each other. You can't transition to an open and sharing world within a closed and selfish system. This naturally leads to dictatorship and fascism. However, to assume that transitioning to a system with similar ideals would always descend into fascism is to oversimplify and misunderstand the drivers and influences of social systems. It is naïve at best and malevolent at worst. Transitioning to a system like communism while still using money is analogous to driving a Formula 1 car with diesel. It doesn't matter how well designed a given system is, with the wrong fuel it will always fail eventually.

If you want to transition to a collective society you need transparency and equality rather than secrecy and power. The internet enables a logistical system that provides transparency of resource distribution and prevents an elite strata of individuals gaming the system for their own benefit. It fosters the necessary trust and fairness to make a system like this work.

7.13. Possibilities for an individual country to transition today

The transition plan described is an idealistic approach that assumes we ditch money in one fell swoop. Our hypothetical transition was played out on a global scale because a Resource Based System is fundamentally a global system. It is a species-level system, not a country-level system. It's unlikely to happen without a smaller-scale test first though.

A resource based country could emerge as a precursor to a global transition. That might occur in a small, innovative, progressive, and largely self-sufficient nation like Costa Rica, Portugal, New Zealand, or Denmark. This would require widespread awareness of the possibilities of a society without money. Unfortunately, they're not remotely close to achieving that today.

The same transition approach could be followed if a single country transitioned. They would produce an abundance within their borders and become a net exporter with a considerable surplus. This would provide a monetary income to import resources they couldn't produce themselves. The money could also be used by their own citizens to travel to monetary countries. The resource based country could allow tourists coming in as well. This would demonstrate the benefits of a Resource Based System in a real world setting. Tourists would experience a society where everything was free and abundant (naturally, visas would have to be carefully managed). This could create the groundswell of support to institute a global transition.

Regardless if the decision to transition is made at a national or global level, we face the same broad challenges in actually arriving at such a decision. These will be covered in Chapter 10.

8. HOW MIGHT THIS SOCIETY SHAPE US?

8.1. Introduction

All life on Earth - for the past 4 billion years - has been in a fight for survival[394]. Now for the first time in the history of life on Earth we have the opportunity to create conditions in which life can exist differently. We can create conditions of abundance and co-operation rather than scarcity and competition. Living in conditions like this would radically alter the nature of our nature. This is a tantalising prospect and we're privileged to be alive at this transcendent epoch – the first time in 4 billion years of biological evolution that a living being has progressed to a level of intellect and technology that mean it no longer has to compete to survive.

Quote
Gabor Mate – Developmental Psychologist
"The myth in our society is that people are competitive, individualistic, and selfish by nature. The reality is quite the opposite. The only way you can talk about human nature concretely is by recognising there are certain human needs. For example, we have a human need for companionship - to be loved, to be attached, to be accepted, to be seen, and to be received for who we are. If those needs are met we develop into people who are compassionate, who are co-operative, and who have empathy for other people. What we see in society today is the distortion of human nature, precisely because so few people have their needs met"

Our behaviour is largely conditioned by our environment. We cannot change it with rules, laws, or political messages. Changes in human nature will arise as a by-product of the design and organisation of our social system. While these changes would be increasingly noticeable with every day that passes after the transition, our generation wouldn't experience the full effect of these changes.

Before we start, let's re-cap the ways the Monetary System shapes us:

---

394 http://www.pnas.org/content/early/2015/10/14/1517557112

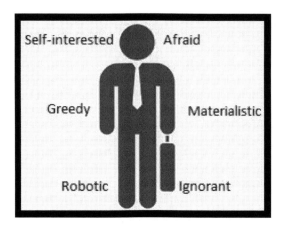

- Self-interested: With scarce resources there is an overwhelming focus on self-interest
- Afraid: With everyone out for themselves we live in a state of perpetual fear
- Greedy: With not enough for everyone we chase limitless money which compromises our character
- Materialistic: With ownership essential for survival we end up valuing material things more than people
- Robotic: With disciplined workers needed we learn to follow procedures rather than think for ourselves
- Ignorant: With such an insular perspective we fail to understand the way our world works

8.2. Collectively-interested, not self-interested

Today – with an inbuilt scarcity – we're compelled to act in regard to our own self-interest first. We must individually earn money to survive. This individualistic focus obfuscates the wasteful consumption of the very resources we need to support human life. It highlights a remarkable situation whereby we're so focused on surviving individually that we're oblivious to the fact we're killing ourselves collectively. Stop and consider the irony of this situation.

Quote
Robert Sapolsky – Neuroendocrinologist
"Different large societies can be termed as individualist or collectivist and you get very different people and different mindsets and different brains coming along with that"

Today we're self-interested and individualistic. In a Resource Based System we'd become collectively-interested and altruistic. That's because all the goods, services, and prosperity we enjoy is owed to our combined efforts. This is in stark contrast to today's world where the goods, services, and prosperity we enjoy is owed primarily to the size of our own bank accounts. This subtle shift in our social circumstance would naturally make us more reliant on others, more understanding of others, and more connected to others. By changing the recipe of our social system we change ourselves. We become more collectively-interested than self-interested.

Psychology and neuroscience are now bursting with evidence of the benefits of sharing, co-operation, and generally behaving in regard to the collective-interest. We know it makes us emotionally happier, physically healthier, enables better relationships, and is also contagious.[395,396]

8.3. Comfortable, not afraid

Today - with everyone out for themselves - it's difficult to trust others. We become afraid of the agendas of other people. This stresses us out, is detrimental to our health, and inhibits our enjoyment of life. We're too afraid to challenge the status quo so we live a life of work with little opportunity to engage in productive pursuits of our own choosing.

In a mature Resource Based System - with abundance and automation - we'd have the comfort and time to follow our dreams, pursue our passions, and dedicate our energies and skills to worthwhile causes that matter to us.

Since ancient times human beings have sought more than just subsistence and survival. They were looking for purpose in their lives. It's no different today. We wonder to ourselves, should I follow my dreams and find a meaningful career? Or should I do something more practical that's sure to pay the bills? We can resolve this dilemma by recognising there are two types of work: economic work and non-economic work. Economic work is effectively a job. Non-economic work is leisure and learning, things that

395http://www.plosone.org/article/fetchArticle.action?articleURI=info:doi/10.1371/journal.pone.0001897
396 http://greatergood.berkeley.edu/article/item/5_ways_giving_is_good_for_you

elevate the mind, things that have a transcendent purpose.

The idealistic notion is this: We do economic work to give us more time for non-economic work (we do jobs to enable leisure and learning). Unfortunately, the opposite happens today. School (non-economic work) serves as a stepping stone to the job market (economic work). We work so much at our menial jobs that we just want to switch off during weekends and vacations. We're too worn out to engage in meaningful non-economic activities. The result is a saddening cycle of robotically living to work. This marginalises the fact that self-directed learning and leisure for their own sake is what gives our lives meaning and purpose[397].

How many people would lead their lives the way they do today if money was no object? Almost nobody would do their job for five days a week if they could do anything they wanted. Few of us have the luxury to discover our own unique talents, abilities, passions, or interests - let alone fulfil them.

Quote
Neil deGrasse Tyson - Astrophysicist
"The great tragedy today is that people are employed in ways that don't fully tap everything they do best in life. If everyone had the luxury of expressing their own unique combinations of talents in the world, then our society would be transformed overnight"

8.4. Humanitarian, not greedy

Today there isn't enough stuff for everyone so we must look out for ourselves first. We're measured by our wealth and there's no upper limit to how much wealth we can acquire. Once we do acquire wealth and power we become self-righteous - we lie, cheat, steal, and corruption is all pervasive. Our greedy culture has compromised our values.

In a mature Resource Based System, without private ownership, scarcity, self-interest, and competition, the concept of trying to get as much as possible for ourselves would fade into obscurity. Without a notion of earning more money to make our own lives better, the systemic recipe

---

397https://www.youtube.com/watch?v=lXnQKrILNpM&list=PL04L9Hu_VHHzfUWruP94IPoKm4kqq4c RH&index=5

that produces greed today disappears.

Studies are beginning to show we're soft wired for humanitarian characteristics like empathy, sociability, and companionship more so than things like greed, self-interest, and materialism. Our brains and nervous systems are tuned to palpably experience the experiences of others around us and respond to others in need.[398,399] Our physiology is inherently geared up for humanitarianism. If we wish to promote it we need to move to a world that enables it to flourish and not be overwhelmed by competing instincts. Humanitarianism tangibly increases things like giving, kindness, sharing, and co-operation[400].

Research

Psychologists analysed the differences between meaning and happiness in people of all ages. They found that leading a happy life is associated with being a taker while leading a meaningful life corresponds with being a giver. Happiness without meaning characterizes a relatively selfish life, in which things go well, needs and desires are easily satisfied, and difficult or taxing entanglements are avoided. People with high meaning in their lives tend to help others in need, whereas those who are happy without meaning tend to look out for themselves.

The psychologists give an evolutionary explanation for this: happiness is about drive reduction. If you have a need or desire - like hunger - you satisfy it, and that makes you happy. Animals have these desires too and when those drives are satisfied, animals also feel happy. What sets human beings apart from animals is not the pursuit of happiness, which occurs all across the natural world, but the pursuit of meaning, which is unique to humans.[401]

When we work for ourselves to earn money (like we do in the Monetary System) we're essentially working for happiness, something that's more evolutionarily primitive and less rewarding than meaning. When we engage in self-directed productive pursuits that benefit the collective-interest (like we would in a Resource Based System), we develop meaning

---

398 https://www.thersa.org/discover/videos/rsa-animate/2010/05/rsa-animate---the-empathic-civilisation/
399 http://greatergood.berkeley.edu/article/item/the_compassionate_instinct
400 https://hbr.org/2011/07/the-unselfish-gene
401 http://faculty-gsb.stanford.edu/aaker/pages/documents/SomeKeyDifferencesHappyLifeMeaningfulLife_2012.pdf

in our lives. The addition of meaning as a cultural linchpin is one of the most important missing ingredients a Resource Based System would add to our lives. It makes us humanitarians.

8.5. Seeking experiences, not material things

Today – with ownership a cultural imperative - we often love our things more than we love each other. This leaves us permanently discontented as we judge ourselves by the stuff we have and not the lives we lead.

With access and co-operation replacing ownership and competition, a Resource Based System would encourage fulfilling shared experiences rather than the isolating sedentary materialism that dominates today's culture. While we'd still utilise material things and have access to an abundance of them, when we don't own them they don't become defining features of our personal identity. Rather, they become tools to enable rich life experiences we share together. The subtle shift in the way we manage and use the material things in our world would have a profound impact on the human experience.

Over the past decade an abundance of psychology research has shown experiences bring people more happiness than material things[402]. Owning material things as symbols of our status quantifiably diminishes the human experience. If we want to shift our focus from 'having things' to 'sharing experiences', we need to change our social system to one that enables it.

8.6. Curious, not robotic

Today – with regimented schooling, mandatory work, and limited opportunities to be successful outside of the system – we're consigned to a robotic life of accepting the way it is. This inundation starts from a young age where every day around the world there are billions of parents telling billions of children the answers: We tell our kids: "There's no such thing as a free lunch", when we should be encouraging them to ask "How could we provide a free lunch for everyone?" We tell our kids: "You need to work hard to earn your living", when we should be encouraging them to ask "How could we utilise technology to free ourselves of the need to

---

402 http://www.theatlantic.com/business/archive/2014/10/buy-experiences/381132/

work and improve our quality of life?"

Quote
Carl Sagan – Cosmologist
"We make our world significant by the courage of our questions and the depth of our answers"

In a Resource Based System there's no requirement for a life of specialised work so there's no requirement for education to train us to work. Without the need for regimented schooling (we'll explore this further in the next chapter) our innate curiosity, creativity, and originality could flourish and we'd be questioning everything.

With a renewed thirst for discovery, we'd gain the humility to accept the things we don't know. We'd recognise that being wrong about something is not shameful or embarrassing, rather, it provides a new level of understanding and increases our awareness of the world around us and our standing within it.

Quote
Joseph Joubert – Moralist; Essayist
"The aim of argument, or of discussion, should not be victory, but progress"

8.7. Engaged, not ignorant

Today our quality of life is influenced more by our individual earnings than the state of our society. Consequently we're far more invested in our own success than our society's'. We disengage from society and become ignorant of the way it works. This vast apathy drives widespread misinformed opinions which disjoint and divide us further.

In a Resource Based System we'd be engaged in our society, precisely because our quality of life depends directly on our society rather than anything we individually achieve. A by-product of being engaged in our society is we educate ourselves on it too - we'd naturally want to understand how everything works. We'd be more aware of our circumstance than we are today.

Thought experiment
Think about something you're personally engaged in today, whether it be a favourite musician, favourite sports team, or favourite TV show.

Chances are you have a comprehensive understanding about that thing or person you're engaged in. That's because when we're engaged in something we naturally educate ourselves on it.

8.8. Comparing the Monetary System and Resource Based System

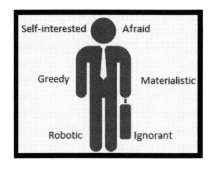 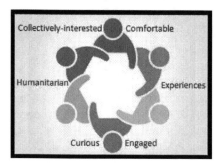

- •Selfish: It's all about me
- •Afraid: Of everyone's agendas
- •Greedy: Chasing wealth & power
- •Materialistic: Having things
- •Robotic: Following procedures
- •Ignorant: Of the big picture

- • Collective: Working together
- • Comfortable: To follow our dreams
- • Humanitarian: Helping others
- • Seeking experiences: Doing things
- • Curious: Questioning everything
- • Engaged: In our social world

There is tremendous potential for both good and bad in human nature. Much of the bad in our nature today can be traced to the bad in our cultural environment. If we want to minimise the bad and encourage the good we need to change our social system to one that promotes the positivity rather than the negativity.

Promoting positivity doesn't mean it would all be positive though. People would still behave badly. For example, today we're encouraged to be self-interested before thinking of others. Despite this, countless people still look out for others - even with no immediate benefit to themselves - whether it be volunteering for a charity or helping the old lady next door take out her garbage. There is a selfless side to our nature that shines through in spite of our selfish system.

Conversely, a Resource Based System encourages us to focus on the collective good. Despite this, some people would still act in regard to their own interest. We're complex beings, we're not always selfless nor are we always selfish. There's no such thing as a perfect world where everyone behaves selflessly 100% of the time. That's not what a Resource Based System is. It's just a system designed to bring out the best in us. A system that promotes the positivity in human nature rather than the negativity.

Behaviours and values are not absolute or unchanging, they operate on a continuum. The positioning of our behaviour on those continuums is not absolute either, it can be shifted by shifting the social environment in which we exist. By changing our social system we change the way most people behave most of the time. We can think of this as shifting the bell curve of human behaviour.

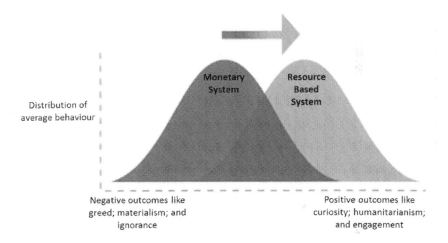

A Resource Based System wouldn't be utopia. It'd just serve to shift the bell curve of human behaviour. The common characteristics of people in any social system are by-products of the design and organisation of that social system. By changing our system we change ourselves.

If the evidence presented so far isn't enough, watch a few documentaries on isolated modern day tribes and you'll begin to understand the mind-boggling palette of possible behavioural "norms" that human beings are capable of.

9. WHAT SITUATIONS MIGHT EMERGE IN THIS SOCIETY?

9.1. Introduction

If we transitioned to a Resource Based System, achieved an abundance, achieved automation, and had a society of people who'd only known that world, what situations would they create? How would those situations differ to the situations we experience today?

This may seem trivial, given none of us alive today would ever experience it in its totality. However, if we decide to re-design our social world, we need to know what that means for future generations. What kind of world would our grandchildren, and their grandchildren, be living in?

This section is a little speculative because it's impossible to know what would happen in a world we have no experience of. While it's speculative that doesn't mean it's unsubstantiated though. We can logically deduce likely situations based on the structure of the social system and the types of people that system would create.

Before we start, let's recap the situations that've emerged in the Monetary System:

- Voting – Is so complex and boring we don't know what we're voting for
- Politicians – Serve the interests of the wealthy ahead of the interests of society
- War – Is an inevitable consequence of scarcity and self-interest
- Laws – Create further inequality, division, and crime
- Crime – Is committed by poor people rather than bad people
- Justice – Does not get served when we focus on punishment ahead of understanding
- Health – Is a privilege enjoyed by the wealthy

9.2. Voting & Politicians

Political information today is complicated and boring. Consequently, few of us understand what we're actually voting for and the idea of democracy loses credibility. It doesn't really matter who we vote for though because most political decisions are made in the interests of the wealthy rather than the interests of society. Our leaders exist as puppets for the wealthy, shaping a future where the rich get richer and the poor get poorer.

Quote

Thomas Jefferson – Founding Father of the United States
"The issue today is the same as it has been throughout history, whether man shall be allowed to govern himself or be ruled by a small elite"

In a Resource Based System – with abundant resources and no countries or money – we wouldn't need politicians in the traditional sense. Making resources abundant is not a political question, it is a logistical question.

There'd still be many situations requiring decisions though, such as moral issues, ethical issues, preferences, disputes, or other sensitivities raised from new ways of doing things. In an engaged and educated social system these would probably be addressed in something resembling a true democracy.

In a true democracy we wouldn't vote for a leader then delegate all decision making responsibility to that leader. Instead we'd probably vote on specific things ourselves. It could be done with a simple app. We'd use the app to read a description of the issue and place our vote. Any subjects too specialised for average citizens could be made by a consortium of experts with their justification made public (in line with the open-source model).

The accepted narrative today is that politicians don't involve citizens directly in decision making because the decisions are too complex. While there is some truth to that (we do indeed have complexity in politics), that complexity only exists because we live in a society based on money. In a society based on money there are vested interests, private agendas, and selfish motivations that need to be considered. In a world without money this complexity is stripped away.

With an engaged and educated population in a world without monetary complexity, there's no reason we couldn't have an informed say on most important matters. Furthermore, we'd have the time and intelligence to place informed votes. The abundance, collectivism, and engagement in a Resource Based System could support a truly democratic process. Consequently, we'd end up with a largely self-governing society.

While we wouldn't need any traditional forms of government to achieve a true democracy like this, we would need people performing some sort of administrative roles. These roles would be in a supporting capacity rather than the controlling capacity of government today.

9.3. War

Almost all wars throughout history were influenced by our inbuilt scarcity, inequality, and greed.

Without a nationalistic system grounded in scarcity, war as we know it today would be unlikely. With a collective focus and equal access to an abundance of resources, the likelihood of war is dramatically reduced. Additionally, in an equal, engaged, and humanitarian society, mobilising one group of people to harm another group of people for self-interested political agendas seems far less likely.

While an equal, engaged, and humanitarian society would be less susceptible to misunderstandings or violent disagreements, they would inevitably still happen (there's no such thing as a perfect world). When they do happen we'd also be better equipped to deal with them though. Why? Because in a society like this we're aware of the perspective of others and learn to respect the perspective of others. This type of empathic society would be naturally equipped to resolve disagreements more effectively than we do today.

9.4. Laws & Crime

Today we have a complex sea of laws and many people employed to enforce the laws – from police officers to lawyers to security guards to judges. Most of these laws only serve to create more crime, inequality, and division, turning poor people into bad people.

Quote
Isaac Asimov – Biochemist, Author
"It is insulting to imply that only a system of rewards and punishments can keep you a decent human being"

While rules, laws, and policing would still be required during the transition, they'd probably lose relevance over time. Rules and laws are ineffective in controlling behaviour because they make us feel trapped into particular ways of doing things. Furthermore, rules and laws are easily broken by those who wish to break them.

Case study

The War on Drugs in the U.S demonstrates the futility of trying to condition human behaviour with laws. It's been one of the biggest policy failures in U.S political history. At the other end of the spectrum we have Portugal's approach to preventing drug abuse - decriminalising all drugs and re-directing money spent on drug enforcement toward education for the young, rehabilitation for the addicted, freedom of choice for everyone, and punishment or incarceration of very few. Drug abuse in Portugal has almost vanished while in the U.S it continues to get worse. Being educated, engaged, and fulfilled is now provably the most effective way to prevent drug abuse. Rules and laws are ineffective in conditioning human behaviour. A supporting social system works far better.

In a Resource Based System it's unlikely we'll need police officers, security guards, or lawmakers. These jobs are necessary when there isn't enough stuff for everyone and everyone is out for themselves. However, in an abundant society we don't need to compete to survive, so almost all rules, laws, and policing become redundant.

A Resource Based System would be largely self-policing. We'd all be "police officers", not because we're paid to but because we're engaged in our society, aware of how it functions, and feel a collective sense of pride and responsibility for the abundance and quality of life it provides. In a society like this we'd each become guardians, not just of our own stuff, but of all stuff. We'd move from a world of countless rules, laws, regulations, and controls - but replete with chaos, to a world with almost no laws, rules, regulations, or controls - that's far more civilised. Crime would be drastically reduced, not by laws, but by eliminating the primary motivations for crime.

9.5. Justice

When someone commits a heinous crime today, we have a tendency to say "lock them up and throw away the key" or "execute them", as if this constitutes some sort of justice. This is a puerile way to address unwanted human behaviours. While it ensures one person won't repeat their heinous crime, whatever caused them to commit the crime will again cause other people to commit similar crimes. Locking someone up does nothing to ensure the heinous crime won't be repeated by others.

In a Resource Based System, justice would probably involve studying the criminals and the situations that led them to commit crimes. That's because as sure as the sun will rise tomorrow, if we exist in the same social circumstance we will have the same behaviours. This isn't to say we wouldn't admonish those who do bad things. However, justice would probably focus more on research and rehabilitation than punishment. This is an approach we know to be more effective.

Case study

In Norway this approach to justice is already being implemented. Prisons are comforting environments that respect human dignity. Even in maximum security prisons, each inmate has their own cells (with their own key), they have their own bathrooms, their own showers, they're actively encouraged to focus on creative pursuits, they have a massive library, and they're allowed to vote like regular citizens. The principle here is, while a prisoner may have made a bad decision they're still a human being and deserve to be treated like one. Furthermore, when someone commits a crime it's often more a reflection of the society than the individual anyway.

In Norway the maximum sentence is 21 years. With this in mind it becomes a collective responsibility to develop prisons with the best chance of rehabilitating the prisoners. That's because sooner or later, every prisoner will re-enter society and when they do they could be your neighbour. The results of this approach are formidable with only 20% recidivism in Norway (which compares to 80% recidivism in the more traditional U.S prison system). Norway also has the lowest murder rate in the world.

Today we tend to see the criminal as an evil wrong-doer and want them to be punished. In a Resource Based System we'd probably sympathise with the criminal as an unfortunate victim of circumstance (the circumstance referring to the subconscious influences on their behaviour). Rather than just punish them, we'd also want to learn from them (to prevent similar crimes in future) and help them (as a fellow human being).

Only one of these notions of justice is actually just. The other is a severe shortcoming in our courage to face up to the underlying causes of our behaviour. In a Resource Based System we'd have justice in the interests of human kind rather than justice in the interests of an individual victim.

9.6. Health

Today our physical health, mental health, quality of life, and length of life are all significantly influenced by the amount of money we have. The majority of people are too poor to enjoy the level of health that we – as a species – are capable of providing for everyone. To make matters worse, our health is largely out of our control, it hinges on our luck in the birth lottery.

In a Resource Based System, a high standard of physical and mental health is enabled for all. That's because we have an abundance of resources, equal opportunity, the removal of the drudgery of work, and the freedom to express ourselves. Even with a higher quality of life we'd still inevitably get sick though. However, when that did happen we'd have access to the highest quality healthcare. Why? Because the primary focus of our social system is utilising technology to enable our well-being. Health is essential for our well-being, therefore high quality healthcare is made abundantly available for all. It would be one of the first things we make abundant.

9.7. Summary

A Resource Based System is an emergent system whereby we all choose the way we live our lives. With this in mind, it seems likely we'd create social conditions where we're not directed, controlled, or enslaved by established institutions. It seems likely we'd foster healthy situations that serve our physical needs, emotional needs, and motivations.

Voting

- Is boring and misunderstood
- Is clear and collaborative

Politicians

- Serve the wealthy
- Don't exist. We self-govern

War

- Is perpetual due to scarcity
- Is unlikely due to abundance

Laws

- Create more crime
- Don't exist. We self-regulate

Crime

- Is committed by poor people
- Is less likely with abundance

Justice

- Seeks mainly to punish
- Focuses on understanding

Health

- Is a privilege for the wealthy
- Is a basic provision for all

While it may be too late for our generation to enjoy a world like this, it's not too late for future generations - as yet unborn - to enjoy a world like this. While we're not mentally equipped to self-govern or self-police today, future generations who'd grown up in a Resource Based System would be.

Once again, this may sound like some sort of unachievable Utopian future but it's not. A Resource Based System can realistically be transitioned into today. Not only that, it's far more compatible with our physiology, our needs, and our motivations than the painful existence we're putting ourselves through today.

9.8. Life in a Resource Based System

To conclude this speculative chapter about people's lives in a future Resource Based System, we'll explore something known by Sociologists as our life script[403]. We're all pretty familiar with the life script today - it's the way most of us have seen our parents live their lives and how many of us intend to live ours. In a nutshell, our life script is:

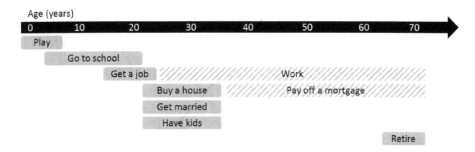

Most of us don't give this too much thought. We see it as a natural course of events. It's not natural though – it's a product of the cultural foundations of the Monetary System. We do these things because we're born into a society where they're culturally relevant. Without money they'd probably lose relevance though. Let's think about our life script today and consider how it might differ in a mature Resource Based System.

Play

Young children have the capacity to learn and understand complex subjects, crucial for reaching their full potential as adults[404,405,406]. Despite

403http://www.academia.edu/6393031/Historical_Research_on_Cultural_Life_Scripts._An_Explorati on_of_Opportunities_and_Future_Prospects_in_Historical_Social_Research_39_2014_1_7-18
404 Learning together: Children and adults in a school community; Rogoff B; ISBN 978-0-19-516031-4, Oxford University Press 2002
405 http://unesdoc.unesco.org/images/0014/001474/147499e.pdf
406 Young children learning; Tizard B & Hughes M; 2002

this, the first years of our lives today are dominated by cartoons, fairy tales, magical stories, mystical worlds, and illusions. We saturate our kids with things like Santa Claus, the Tooth Fairy, and the Easter Bunny.

We raise our kids on a foundation of lies, and then hypocritically, expect them to be honest when they grow up. What kind of foundation is that on which to start a life? We see our kids smiling and laughing at these stories so it seems like we're being nice to them. We're not though. While cultivating their imagination is critical, we shackle their growth if we overwhelm them with lies and don't provide sufficient opportunities for cognitive development.

In a mature Resource Based System - without a prolonged period of mind-numbing working slavery up ahead – playtime wouldn't need to be crammed into a few years of childhood. People would be playing and having fun their entire lives. It seems likely the formative years of childhood would be more appropriately balanced between playing, having fun, and having opportunities to think critically and develop cognitively. This would produce a society of adults far better equipped to understand their reality, address the challenges they face, and lead fulfilling lives.

Go to school

Today our schools groom us for the robotic work that's required. They focus on rote memorisation, standardised testing, and following procedures. These things aid in the development of a disciplined menial worker, precisely the type of adult that's needed. Unfortunately, spending too much time in regimented schools hinders the development of cognitive skills such as organisation, long-term planning, self-regulation, task initiation, and the ability to switch between activities[407].

In a Resource Based System, a less prescriptive educational approach would probably emerge. We'd be naturally curious and engaged so we wouldn't need to prescribe learning, we'd just want to enable it. How do we enable learning? We teach kids how to learn about things that interest them.

If a child is fascinated with the microstructure of a flower we introduce them to botany, if they're mesmerised by the stars we introduce them to astronomy, if they're intrigued by bridges we introduce them to

---

407 http://journal.frontiersin.org/article/10.3389/fpsyg.2014.00593/full

engineering. Most importantly, we do it right then as something piques their curiosity. We don't just feed them information though, we teach them how to critically evaluate information. We also teach them about their own cognitive biases and how to solve problems. This ensures they can learn for themselves in the present moment, but also, can learn about anything, anytime, for the remainder of their lives. It also ensures they're equipped to address the challenges they face, both individually and collectively.

In this way education becomes a supporting framework rather than a controlling framework. We cultivate the cognitive ability that exists in all humans to critically evaluate information themselves. If we develop these skills at a young age, is prescriptive and mandatory schooling still relevant?

Thought experiment
Why do we pay for schooling? Why do we pay to go to university? Are we paying for the privilege of receiving information we couldn't get elsewhere? No. All the information we learn in any university course, plus mountains more, is available for free to anyone with an internet connection.

Anyone with an internet connection - coupled with an ability to think for themselves - could become a world leading expert in any given field without ever attending school. Today we don't learn to think for ourselves though. Instead we go to school or university to learn the things our teachers tell us. We're not required to assess the things they tell us, we're just required to recite them. This delegation of intellectual responsibility is fraught with danger and produces robotic, unquestioning minds.

Research
Researchers put computers with high speed internet in the walls of slums in many countries around the world, then walked away. Kids in these countries had never seen a computer before. With no supervision or guidance, kids found the computers, learnt how to use them, and taught themselves all manner of things - from maths, to speaking English, to making music, to learning complex subjects. This happened through being challenged, through collaborating, and through a self-directed learning and thinking process.

The findings from a wide range of similar studies around the world were that:

1. Children will learn to do what they want to learn to do
2. Groups of children can learn to use a computer on their own, irrespective of who or where they are
3. Groups of children can navigate the internet to achieve educational objectives on their own
4. Groups of children learning together retain information better than groups being told by a teacher[408]

Case study

In global education rankings, Finland is constantly near the top. This success is the product of drastic changes to their education system. They now have the shortest school day, the shortest school year, and no homework. Recognising the benefits of self-directed study or play, they've reduced the mandatory component of education. This is producing more intellectually and emotionally mature adults.

There's a perception in most countries that without regimented schooling, kids would just play and learn nothing. All the research suggests this perception is misguided and founded in the established ways of a system trying to condition its people to work and follow rules rather than fostering an environment in which they can learn[409,410].

Research

A group of schools in New Zealand tested the effect of removing rules in the playground for two years. Kids would do things like climb trees, ride scooters and skateboards, play with old tyres and junk in a "loose parts pit", and have mud fights - all things that would have been against the rules normally.

This led to a number of unexpected and beneficial by-products. It kept kids out of trouble, decreased bullying, decreased vandalism, reduced serious injuries, and increased concentration levels in class. They became motivated, busy, and engaged by having the autonomy to do what they wanted. Researchers found the great paradox of over-protecting children

408 http://www.ted.com/talks/sugata_mitra_the_child_driven_education?language=en#t-977955
409 http://www.theatlantic.com/magazine/archive/2014/04/hey-parents-leave-those-kids-alone/358631/
410 http://www.goodreads.com/book/show/15843125-free-to-learn

is more dangerous in the long run as it ignores the benefits of risk taking. Children develop the frontal lobe of their brain when taking risks, meaning they work out consequences. You can't teach them that, they have to learn risk on their own terms.[411]

Schools like we have today seem unlikely in a Resource Based System. What seems more likely is places to learn about things that interest us. Interactive learning centres - enabling people to both think for themselves and learn together - seem more likely than schools. The result would be a largely self-educating society where we learn from one another and with one another. It would be a society in which learning is a lifelong endeavour, enabling fulfilment and stimulation throughout life. This 'whole-of-life' approach to education is well supported by scientific studies that show learning boosts happiness at all ages, not just while growing up[412,413].

If we want an educated society we must first have an engaged society. If we want an engaged society we must first have a motivated society. If we want a motivated society we must first have the comfort to follow our dreams. In a Resource Based System, all of these pre-requisites are met. They enable a society where we can largely self-educate. In a Resource Based System, education would probably be based around[414]:

1. Providing all who want to learn with access to available resources at any time in their lives
2. Empowering all who want to share what they know to find those who want to learn it from them
3. Furnishing all who want to present an issue to the public with the opportunity to do so
4. Using modern technology to make free speech, free assembly, and a free press truly universal and therefore fully educational.

Get a job

Today we're removed from school around age 18. We then dedicate ourselves to work because we must, in order to survive. We specialise in a given field and focus on it our entire lives, a concept known as a career.

411 http://tvnz.co.nz/national-news/school-ditches-rules-and-loses-bullies-5807957
412 http://psycnet.apa.org/index.cfm?fa=buy.optionToBuy&id=1978-23415-001
413 http://greatergood.berkeley.edu/article/item/can_an_online_course_boost_happiness
414 http://www.preservenet.com/theory/Illich/Deschooling/intro.html

Many of us dive into these careers without too much thought. We take off on this linear trajectory, building our careers, often without considering what we really want in life or what excites us. In some cases people may want to dedicate their whole lives to one specialisation but it shouldn't be the default, particularly given the majority of our careers don't reflect our personal interests or passions.

In a world designed for our well-being we recognise this for what it is - an outdated and harmful situation. In a Resource Based System, we'd spend our lives following our passions and doing whatever stimulates us.

Get married

For 99% of our time, marriage didn't exist. Marriage arose along with money and originally had nothing to do with love. Instead, it was used for the protection of bloodlines and property[415]. From then onward it was a financial arrangement, whereby a man provided financial security for the bride. Only since the 19th century has it become about love in some parts of society and in many parts of the world today it's still a financial arrangement[416]. The correlation between marriage and love is a cultural manifestation of modern Western society.

70% of marriages end in divorce, separation, or devolve into bitterness and dysfunction[417]. The 30% of marriages that do work are shown to be among more accommodating people who compromise their own values to make it work. Few couples remain completely suitable for each other forever[418]. That's because we're not static beings. We change enormously through every phase of our lives.

Research

This longitudinal study examines how people change over the next 10 years of their life vs how they think they'll change. The study shows we grossly underestimate how much our values, beliefs, opinions, and preferences will change over the next 10 years of our lives, regardless of our current age. We see the present moment as this watershed on the timeline, the moment in which we've finally become ourselves. We

415 http://marriage.about.com/cs/generalhistory/a/marriagehistory.htm
416 http://en.wikipedia.org/wiki/Weddings_in_the_United_States
417 http://tytashiro.net/the-science-of-happily-ever-after/
418 http://www.businessinsider.com/lasting-relationships-rely-on-2-traits-2014-11

struggle to perceive we'll change much from the finished article we believe we are today.[419]

Thought experiment

Think back to your childhood best friend - the friend you had the strongest connection with. Is that person still your best friend today? For some of you they may be but for most of you they won't. That's because over time you changed in different ways. You developed a stronger connection with someone else. As the above study shows, these changes aren't just confined to growing up. We change enormously throughout our entire lives.

So let's think about marriage now. We get married when we find someone we have a strong connection with. Over time we change, we always have and always will. Sooner or later, we meet someone else we have a stronger connection with. This time it's different though. It's not like our friendships. We can't shift to a new partner like we have with our friends. We're married.

Why did we enter into this life-long social contract though? Especially if this contract could prevent further enriching experiences with others in the future? After all, the joy of being alive as a living conscious being is something we should all treasure and seek to maximise, not restrict.

The idea of a life-long social contract isn't that compatible with our changing nature[420,421,422]. So why do we do it? Aside from it being the cultural norm, we do it because marriage enables so much today:

- Two incomes enables better management of expenses and financial security
- Two incomes enables the purchase of a house, which for many is unaffordable with one income
- Having a "guaranteed for life" companion means we're not on our own, there's someone in it with us

---

419 https://www.youtube.com/watch?v=XNbaR54Gpj4
420 http://danielbergner.com/what-do-women-want/
421 http://www.audible.com/pd/Erotica-Sexuality/Mating-in-Captivity-Audiobook/B002V8HNWC/ref=a_search_c4_1_1_srTtl/185-7293323-7477401?qid=1417816959&sr=1-1
422 http://www.ted.com/talks/christopher_ryan_are_we_designed_to_be_sexual_omnivores#t-122005

In a Resource Based System, legally locking down one person to love for life would probably lose relevance. It seems likely we'd enter into more flexible arrangements that accommodate the way we change.

Buy a house

Once we've chosen our partner we purchase our nest and settle down. Settling down is not innate in our nature though[423]. Buying a house and settling down is a reflection of our culture – a materialistic culture based on ownership and status. The house we buy and settle in becomes a symbol of our status. Today many of us buy a house and settle down just because we believe it's part of growing up.

For some though it's not a choice. Settling down is the only affordable option. Being settled comes with many financial advantages around surety of income and managing expenses. To lead a life of adventure and exploration is prohibitively expensive for the majority of people.

In a Resource Based System - without the cultural and financial shackles - its likely people would lead more adventurous, exploratory, and fulfilling lives. The idea of saving up to buy a house and spending our lives paying off a mortgage would not exist. Without desires for ownership and status, the materialistic and sedentary lifestyle would surely be far less favoured. Some would still lead settled lives but that would be a choice for each of us, free of the financial constraints that exist today.

Have kids

Today the act of giving birth is celebrated and congratulated almost without exception. It's a cultural tradition widely considered to be a rite of passage. Should it be though?

Thought experiment

How many of us wake up one day and think "I know what we need as a species.. we need more people!". Nobody thinks that, not one of us. The reasons we give birth are predominantly selfish - either we're following the cultural script and trying to fit in, or maybe we feel a child will give our lives purpose, or maybe we want children to look after us when we grow old. In any of these cases, the motivation for having kids is selfish. This is the type of behaviour we'll continue to exhibit so long as we exist in a

---

423 http://books.google.ca/books?id=fkifXu2gx4YC&redir_esc=y

self-interested social system. It's leading to the gross and increasing over-population we experience today.

In a Resource Based System, everyone would be working together as opposed to being out for themselves. Furthermore, people would be engaged in society and educated on the factors that drive it. In this situation, the choice to procreate would probably factor in both the community and species globally, in harmony with personal desires.

With abundance, comfort, and equality, people would likely be less private, less afraid of strangers, and more connected with all others in their communities. Children probably wouldn't be as reliant on their biological parents as their only means of security and their only avenue to learn about the world. Children would probably learn from many different people, gaining a broad range of viewpoints and ideas. This would result in a more well-rounded and grounded society of adults.

Retire

Retiring is something we do once we finish work. With no work in a Resource Based System there would be nothing to retire from. Our entire lives would be free and self-directed. This would enable us to spend time on whatever we choose, whether it be a lot or a little. The concept of retirement – much like the concept of school, jobs, marriages, and mortgages - would be unlikely to exist in a mature Resource Based System.

Summary of life in a Resource Based System

Today we tend to have the lives we can afford rather than the lives we want. We're enslaved by money and the culture it has produced.

In a Resource Based System we wouldn't have this constraint. A Resource Based System empowers us to live how we want by making resources and information abundantly available. It wouldn't determine one way of life, it would enable any way of life. The beauty of human life is we're all different. No two people are the same nor do they wish to live their lives in the same way. In a Resource Based System this fact of human nature is respected. We're not culturally shoehorned to follow a script. Our lives would be what we make of them. It would be a genuine freedom not experienced by any of us today.

Analogy

Today we're constantly chasing that next thing. We go to school to pass the tests and get through the grades. Then we go to university to get our degree and move onto work. At work we seek the next promotion so we can buy the nicer car and the better house. We continue on this journey chasing the next thing as though we'll eventually reach some final destination, at which point we'll be happy.

In a Resource Based System, life would be more like music than it would a journey. Music is not something we listen to to get to the end. We listen to the composition to enjoy the composition. It's the same with dancing, we don't aim to get to a certain point in the room, the whole point of dancing is the dance. Life in a Resource Based System would be less of a scripted journey and more like a piece of dance or music. We'd enjoy life for what it is rather than the non-existent pilgrimage at the end. In a Resource Based System we'd cherish every moment rather than chasing something we never quite reach because it's always one step away.[424]

While the picture painted of a Resource Based System over the last four chapters has been quite detailed, it's by no means unerring gospel. There would be no fixed blueprint in a Resource Based System. The last four chapters have been an exercise in visualising a better social system than our current one. At the heart of a Resource Based System would be a readiness to change, update, and improve. It would be a constantly evolving social system, designed by the people for the people. Adaptability is an inbuilt characteristic of a social system devoid of hierarchy and filled with engaged, curious, and humble people.

9.9. Other popular alternatives to money

Throughout the past four chapters we've been focusing on one alternative only – a Resource Based System. There's many other popular alternatives or supplements to money though:

- A guaranteed base or minimum income for all citizens[425]

---

424 https://www.youtube.com/watch?v=qHnIJeE3LAl
425http://www.policyalternatives.ca/sites/default/files/uploads/publications/reports/docs/CCPA_Guaranteed_Income_Nov_2009.pdf

- A gold standard – ensuring money returns to being based on quantifiable real objects[426]
- An energy standard – meaning money is more tied to our resources better enabling sustainability[427]
- A fixed virtual currency like bitcoin[428]
- An ownership economy[429]
- Measures to reduce inequality such as capping incomes for high earners[430]
- Negative interest money[431]
- Community currencies[432]
- Time-banking[433]
- Collaborative consumption[434]
- Sovereign money[435]

There's a common problem with all these popular alternatives. While they may be slightly fairer, more equitable, and less wasteful than today's Monetary System, they're still all based on a form of exchange. Any system of exchange will always result – to some extent - in self-interest and scarcity, which inevitably leads to waste and degradation. With the current population and strain on resources, these are not feasible.

Quote
Christopher Doll – Sustainability Researcher
"Very often we cannot countenance that the system in which we live may be flawed. We point to all the benefits and try and tweak the system to eliminate the less desirable elements only for another problem to emerge elsewhere. The end result is a perpetual 'whack-a-mole' game where we're forced to innovate quicker than the speed at which 'unforseen' problems appear"

We need a new approach that directly addresses the challenges we face.

---

426 http://en.wikipedia.org/wiki/Gold_standard
427 http://dspace.mit.edu/bitstream/handle/1721.1/2023/SWP-1353-09057784.pdf
428 https://bitcoin.org/en/
429 http://ownershipeconomy.net/
430 http://en.wikipedia.org/wiki/Maximum_wage
431 http://sacred-economics.com/sacred-economics-chapter-12-negative-interest-economics/
432 http://en.wikipedia.org/wiki/Local_currency
433 http://en.wikipedia.org/wiki/Time-based_currency
434 http://www.collaborativeconsumption.com/
435 http://www.sovereignmoney.eu/

Any exchange-based society would be incapable of doing this. We need an abundant society. It doesn't necessarily have to be a Resource Based System exactly as described throughout the last four chapters - it could well be something very different - but it cannot be based on exchanging scarce resources, it must be based on availing abundant resources.

Quote
Buckminster Fuller – Designer, Inventor, Author
"You never change things by fighting the existing reality. To change something, build a new model that makes the existing model obsolete"

10. WHAT DOES THE FUTURE HOLD FOR US?

10.1. Introduction

12,000 years ago we shifted from the nomadic hunter gather lifestyle to the settled agricultural lifestyle. This was the most significant cultural shift in the past few million years of hominid evolution[436]. Today we have the opportunity to proactively institute another cultural shift of that magnitude by moving from a scarce monetary society to an abundant moneyless society. Is this likely to happen though? In this chapter we'll explore:

- How our future might play out if we remain in the Monetary System.
- The challenges we face in agreeing to transition to a moneyless social system.
- The drivers of social change and the prospects of it happening.

While projections about the future are never certain, this doesn't mean they're unsubstantiated. We can make projections based on quantifiable information.

10.2. Learning from history

Quote
Winston Churchill – Former Prime Minister of the United Kingdom
"The farther backward you can look, the farther forward you are likely to see"

We have a fairly good understanding of past human civilisations: rises, falls, trends, changes, events, occurrences, successes, and failures. From the direction of our predecessors we can learn about the direction we're heading.

Over past 3,000 years there are clear phases in the rise and fall of advanced human civilisations. These phases are apparent in almost all past empires - from the Assyrian, to the Persian, to the Greek, to the

---

436 Andrew Hill & Steven Ward (1988). "Origin of the Hominidae: The Record of African Large Hominoid Evolution Between 14 My and 4 My". Yearbook of Physical Anthropology 31 (59): 49–83

Roman, to the Arab, to the Ottoman, to the Spanish, to the Russian, to the British. The same phases have been repeated[437].

What are these phases that past civilisations experienced, from their initial rise to their final fall?

Historical lifecycles of human civilisations

The age of pioneers – Untrammelled by traditions and uninhibited by textbooks, they'll turn anything available to their purpose. They have a readiness to improvise and experiment. Action is their solution to every problem.

The age of conquests – Free to use their own improvisations, they're confident, daring, and optimistic. Schools teach bravery. They conquer land from others, penetrate new forests, climb unexplored mountains, sail uncharted seas.

The age of commerce – The conquest of vast amounts of land across multiple climates naturally stimulates commerce. It enables them to produce varied products across regions and trade with one another.

The age of affluence – Increased production enables prosperity for the masses. They become comfortable. School no longer teaches bravery, it enables people to get rich. Courage and enterprise begin declining.

The age of intellect – School is no longer about wealth accumulation but academic honours. Perceived individual intelligence shifts society to more self-centred values. Intellect destroys unity and community.

The age of decadence – Having conquered all before them, those at the top consolidate power and exhibit audacious displays of wealth. Society turns to mindless entertainment and wasteful luxuries. They become fat and lazy.

The age of decline – Frivolous decadence can't replace the substance of earlier ages. A tiny minority at the top try to persuade the masses the society is still great but people don't feel it anymore. They search for it in food, alcohol, sex, sports, and drugs, but don't find it.

These seven ages within a lifecycle take about ten generations (250 years) on average. What stage is our now globally connected, U.S-led capitalist

---

437 http://www.rexresearch.com/glubb/glubb-empire.pdf

monetary civilisation in? Keep in mind, this is a civilisation that essentially started when the U.S declaration of independence was signed in 1776 (240 years ago).

What stage are we in today?

If it isn't obvious yet, consider also that the heroes of a civilisation reflect the stage of the civilisation. In the initial stages of a civilisation, soldiers, builders, pioneers, and explorers are admired – these are the celebrities. Through the middles stages of a civilisation, businessmen and entrepreneurs are the celebrities. During the last stages of decadence and decline, the celebrities are sports stars, actors, musicians, and chefs. The celebrities and heroes of a civilisation reflect the stage that civilisation is in.

Today we're clearly in a chronic decline. We used to feel great but we don't feel it anymore so we search for it in the greatest food, greatest music, and greatest entertainment. Organisations seeking to provide these things begin to devour the very heritage upon which our civilisation was originally built.

More and more institutions are created and great swathes of the way we live our lives become institutionalized. This process undermines people – it diminishes our confidence in ourselves and in our capacity to solve problems. We cynically give up looking for solutions to the problems which seem too big and impossible to solve[438].

Both irresponsible pleasure-seeking and pessimism increase among the people and their leaders. The military becomes bloated, undisciplined, and over-extended. We see the audacious and conspicuous display of wealth and we see a massive disparity between rich and poor.

The dominant minority of leaders continue to force the majority to obey without meriting obedience. The leaders fail to adequately address the next challenge society faces due to a worship of their "former self", by which they become overly prideful and consequently ignorant of the present[439]. The downward spiral overwhelms the civilisation and it

---

438 Adult Education at the Crossroads: Learning Our Way Out; Finger, Matthias and Asun, Jose Manuel; Published by National Institute of Adult Continuing Education, 2004; ISBN 10: 1862011087 / ISBN 13: 9781862011083
439 http://nobsword.blogspot.ca/1993_10_17_nobsword_archive.html

eventually collapses.

Is the same fate likely to befall us?

Quote

Nick Hanauer – Entrepreneur, Venture Capitalist
"No society can sustain this kind of rising inequality. In fact, there is no example in human history where wealth accumulated like this and the pitchforks didn't eventually come out. You show me a highly unequal society and I will show you a police state or an uprising. There are no counterexamples. None. It's not if, it's when"

Research

A 2014 study by NASA warns that precipitous collapse, often lasting centuries, has been common in societies with conditions like those we have today. In all such cases over the last few thousand years, the continued stretching of resources coupled with a two-classed society (elites and masses) has led to collapse. Modelling a range of different scenarios, NASA concludes that under conditions like those we have today, collapse is difficult to avoid.[440,441]

Further to this, the emerging scientific field of cliodynamics – a transdisciplinary area of research that integrates cultural evolution, economics, and macrosociology to make mathematical models of long term social processes – is unveiling many disturbing findings about our global society today[442].

While our historical analysis doesn't paint a pretty picture, it's not all doom and gloom. There's still cause for optimism. While our current system may be doomed to fail, that doesn't mean we can't proactively transition to another one. We'll examine this later in the chapter.

10.3. Future technologies and threats

Future technologies will bring undreamt opportunities but they'll also concoct new threats. The way we manage these threats will probably define our species. Let's take a closer look at some of the technologies

---

440 http://www.alternet.org/economy/nasa-funded-study-industrial-civilization-headed-irreversible-collapse-due-inequality
441 http://www.sciencedirect.com/science/article/pii/S0921800914000615
442 http://escholarship.org/uc/irows_cliodynamics

and threats.

Nanotechnology

Future nanotechnology is expected to enable us to produce anything we want at around a dollar per kilo[443]. That's a good price for potatoes, wheat, eye fillet steak, or lobster, but what about things like oil, gold, or diamonds? When we can produce diamonds for the same cost as potatoes, it's unlikely we'll view them as jewellery. In fact, when nothing is scarce what will happen to the concept of jewellery? Would it even exist? What would we use diamonds for? Well, diamonds are about 50 times stronger than steel so they'd probably be used in building, space, and aeronautics. Using existing design requirements of single-stage to orbit spaceships, you could build a 60kg diamond car, fill it with the required 3000kg of fuel at a very low cost, and drive your own car directly off the highway up into space.[444]

Such a paradigm shift for a single material wouldn't be unheard of. Aluminium, for example, went through a similar revolution. It used to be a highly sought after material by rich people who used it for their dinner sets as a sign of wealth. Then we discovered the process for making aluminium, now it's a construction material. With nanotechnology it won't just be one material though, it'll be all materials.

The threat here is that nanotechnology makes resources ubiquitous. They become so abundant that money (a system for exchanging scarce resources) becomes fundamentally incompatible. If this technology proliferates rapidly - which it's expected to - the existing bureaucratic control structures of the Monetary System may not be able to adapt quick enough. If it leads to a spectacular and violent collapse, the breakdown of basic infrastructure and societal values could lead to catastrophic loss of human life.

While ubiquitous resources are a threat in the Monetary System, they'd be overwhelmingly positive in a Resource Based System.

Artificial Intelligence

Quote
Stephen Hawking – Theoretical Physicist

---

443 https://www.youtube.com/watch?v=cdKyf8fsH6w
444 https://www.youtube.com/watch?v=cdKyf8fsH6w

"I think the development of full artificial intelligence could spell the end of the human race. Humans - who are limited by slow biological evolution - couldn't compete and would be superseded"

Artificial Intelligence (AI) is intelligence created by humans using machines or computers[445]. 98% of world leading experts believe AI will reach a point of greater-than-human intelligence at some point in the next century and the majority think it will happen before 2050[446]. In other words, it's not a question of if, but when. The biggest question following that is, what will it mean for us? Will it be good or bad? And how can we increase the chances of it being good rather than bad?

The threat here is reaching greater-than-human intelligence without due care and wiping ourselves out - most likely by accident, but possibly by design[447,448,449,450]. The chances of somebody messing something up seems far greater in a self-interested, profit-driven, competitive social system like the Monetary System. We'd all be rushing to do it first to maximise profit, increasing the likelihood of someone getting something wrong[451]. The chances of even just one AI being accidentally hostile (which could be enough to wipe us out) is dramatically increased in a competitive and self-interested monetary society. In a more humanitarian and collectively-focused social system we'd have a better chance of carefully managing it and ensuring it's good for humanity rather than bad.

Immortality

Quote
Aubrey de Grey – Gerontologist
"It is the set of accumulated side-effects of metabolism that eventually kills us"

Aging is a combination of a list of deteriorating conditions that we don't consider to be diseases, such as decline in immune function, loss of muscle, and gain of fat. While we don't always consider the cumulative

445 Eden, Amnon; Moor, James; Søraker, Johnny; Steinhart, Eric, eds. (2013). Singularity Hypotheses: A Scientific and Philosophical Assessment. Springer. p. 1
446 http://fora.tv/2012/10/14/Stuart_Armstrong_How_Were_Predicting_AI
447 http://www.stuff.co.nz/technology/digital-living/63818360/Hawking-thinks-AI-could-end-mankind
448 http://time.com/3614349/artificial-intelligence-singularity-stephen-hawking-elon-musk/
449 http://www.cnet.com/news/stephen-hawking-ai-could-end-humanity/
450 http://www.iflscience.com/technology/scientists-and-engineers-warn-artificial-intelligence
451 http://waitbutwhy.com/2015/01/artificial-intelligence-revolution-1.html

effects of aging to be a disease, that doesn't mean it's something that can't be cured.

Soon we'll be able to prevent the necessity to die of old age. Therapies in development today are already turning off the aging of cells[452]. Other research in stem cells demonstrates we could increase lifespan threefold with a simple injection[453], and yet another piece of research demonstrates we can actually reverse the effects of aging and get younger[454].

Much like a classic car that can have its parts regularly serviced and restored, the human body can also be revitalised. With appropriate funding, world leading experts believe we could be only 50 years away from eliminating aging, living potentially forever[455]. The frontier of immortality is on our doorstep.

The threat here is an exponential spike in population that throws the current over-population well beyond the critical threshold. With our current culture that encourages birth ad nauseam, this could have catastrophic consequences. In a Resource Based System, with a collectively-focused population engaged in their society and educated on the things that matter, we'd be better equipped to manage the impending possibility of immortality and avert the impending disaster of rampant overpopulation.

10.4. Managing threats in the Monetary System

We've just taken a look at three specific technological threats. The underlying question we need to ask in relation to all threats generally is: how well can we manage them in the Monetary System? To understand this we need to consider a couple of things:

1. Are we capable of *acknowledging threats* in the Monetary System?
2. If acknowledged, are we capable of *addressing threats* in the Monetary System?

Acknowledging threats

---

452 http://genesdev.cshlp.org/content/early/2014/09/18/gad.246256.114
453 http://news.nationalgeographic.com/news/2012/01/120106-aging-mice-stem-cells-old-young-science-health/
454 http://hsci.harvard.edu/news/functioning-aged-brains-and-muscles-mice-made-younger
455 http://mfoundation.org/about

We live in a hierarchical society that values being right all the time. Our leaders must always present an image of confidence, stability, and surety. They cannot appear uncertain or vulnerable, regardless if the situation calls for it.

Does an over-confident, self-centred society like this have the humility to acknowledge impending threats? A quick glance at history shows none of our predecessors acknowledged threats until it was too late. This is because the self-maximising, power-driven ways of monetary societies are not conducive to humility.

Anyway, let's just assume for now we do somehow acknowledge threats before it's too late. How would we address these threats in the Monetary System?

Addressing threats

Attempts to prevent these threats would revolve around laws, rules, regulations, tighter controls, removing freedom, and turning the world into more of a police state than it already is. This is a fear-based approach. It's really the only option in an individualistic society. With everyone out for themselves we can't trust people so we must impose tight restrictions on them.

But who wants to live in a world of fear where our every action is monitored because we're all so afraid? And are laws and rules even going to be effective at preventing the types of threats we're likely to face in the future? Laws and rules are routinely and easily broken by those who wish to break them.

Threats are no longer isolated, they're planetary

Quote
Carl Sagan – Cosmologist
"We can't say that one nation can do what it wants within its borders because what you do within one countries borders has consequences all over the planet. There's certainly a chance of getting out of this mess but not by business as usual. There has to be a new way of looking at the future, and that is we're all humans, we're all members of the same species, we're on one fragile little planet, we're all in this together, and we have to work together. The silver lining of all our crises is they're forcing us to become a planetary species"

Throughout history, when threats affected societies it was indeed catastrophic but our planet was still intact. We still had resources and the chance to rebuild and try again. That's because threats in the past were more confined. Societies were more disconnected - what happened in one part of the world didn't significantly affect other parts of the world.

Today we're faced with a radically different proposition. We may not get the chance to try again because our imminent threats are *planetary threats*. They're threats that affect everyone, not just those within the borders of some countries. If a country drops an atomic bomb it doesn't just affect people within the borders of that country, it affects everyone. We're privileged to be alive at this pivotal moment in the history of our species – the first moment in which we've become advanced enough to be a danger to ourselves.

Our fractured, stratified, individualistic, dog-eat-dog society has 198 countries each with their own laws, rules, and controls. This type of society is ill-equipped to acknowledge and address our global threats. Today we seem to view ourselves as an indestructible force. In reality we seem more like a species destined for self-destruction.

We cannot stop our technological capabilities improving but we can change the social system in which we manage them. Our generation are the unwitting custodians of this choice, entrusted with making the necessary change of course for our species.

This may well be a familiar scene playing out throughout the cosmos – life begins and evolves, brains grow larger, intelligence leads to tool making and technology, technology enables abundance, but then, what happens next? Do they outgrow the multi-billion year evolutionary soft-wiring to fight for survival and agree to work together? Or is the basic evolutionary fight for survival so ingrained they continue to look out for themselves, oblivious to the imminent self-destruction of their own species they're collectively overseeing? We do not know the answer to this question. We ourselves are playing in a cosmic drama like this today.

Quote
Carl Sagan – Cosmologist
"There are not yet any obvious signs of extra-terrestrial intelligence. This makes us wonder whether civilizations like ours rush inevitably, headlong toward self-destruction"

A cursory glance at our recent history suggests we may well have been lucky to make it this far. Over the past few decades with things like the Cold War, the Cuban Missile Crisis, and many near misses with powerful technological weapons[456], it's not hard to imagine a different causality scheme whereby we weren't so lucky.

The Doomsday Clock – a measure of our proximity to cataclysmic catastrophe in global society – is currently sitting at three minutes to midnight (in 1991 it was seventeen minutes to midnight)[457]. This is a sobering reminder of our vulnerability and the direction we've been heading over the past couple of decades. Our species is in trouble, make no mistake about it. If we don't chart a new course soon it will be curtains. The fragility of our situation is palpable. The stakes are high.

10.5. Challenges we face in achieving change

We are irrational and emotional beings

A Resource Based System is a practical, rational, logical solution. We humans are emotional beings though, not rational beings[458]. The way we arrive at conclusions, form beliefs, develop biases, inherit values, and process information is organic and idiosyncratic. Despite many of our preconceptions, we're not clinical, truth-seeking, reasoning machines[459].

Case study

This can be seen in the way we donate to diseases. Prostate Cancer has a strong fundraising campaign we can emotionally connect with (Movember). As a result, we donate around $147m per annum to it and it kills around 20,000 people. The three biggest killers are Heart Disease, Diabetes, and Chronic Obstructive Pulmonary Disease. These three kill over 800,000 people (40 times as many as Prostate Cancer) but don't have fundraising campaigns as successful as Movember. Consequently, they raise only $65m combined (less than half of Prostate Cancer).[460]

In a rational society, donations would be proportionate to the amount of

456 http://www.ucsusa.org/nuclear-weapons/close-calls#.WRuCxuWGPIV
457 http://thebulletin.org/timeline
458 https://www.princeton.edu/~achaney/tmve/wiki100k/docs/Cognitive_bias.html
459 http://www.iflscience.com/how-teach-all-students-think-critically
460 http://www.iflscience.com/health-and-medicine/infographic-shows-differences-between-diseases-we-donate-and-diseases-kill-us

suffering the disease causes. Today donations are to diseases with the most appealing fundraising campaigns. These usually target the emotional connection we have with a friend who is involved.

Quote
Alan Watts – Philosopher
"We have a cluster of problems – the question of the population, the question of the pollution of the air and water, the pollution of the Earth itself. What are we going to do about the racial problem? What are we going to do about the poverty programme? How are we going to get rid of work and drudgery without creating the unacceptable problem of unemployment? Every one in itself is a major problem and put together they're so enormous that the mind boggles. However, there is an available known technical solution for every one of these problems - but it's virtually impossible to convince people to do it"

The avoidance of responsibility

We're all aware of most problems in the world, at least to some extent. Crime, inequality, deprivation, hunger, corruption, war, and so on - we all know these things exist. Most of us do nothing about it though. Why not?

Research
An actor lies on the steps of a major passenger thoroughfare at one of London's busiest train stations. The actor moans in pain, clutching their stomach as if seriously ill. Many people walk past, step over the victim, or just appear indifferent to the situation. Others pause for a moment, look around, and then continue on their way. Nobody stops to help for over 30 minutes though. After one person finally stops to help, within seconds many more are crowding round to help too. It wasn't that people didn't notice or didn't want to help in the first 30 minutes, it's just the inclination to conform to the group and not be the initial outlier was too great.[461]

This is known as the Bystander effect – it's been demonstrated in countless situations, countries, and cultures[462,463,464,465]. It states that the

461 http://www.youtube.com/watch?v=OSsPfbup0ac
462 http://www.ncbi.nlm.nih.gov/pubmed/21534650
463http://wadsworth.cengage.com/psychology_d/templates/student_resources/0155060678_rathus/ps/ps19.html
464 http://psycnet.apa.org/journals/psp/19/3/306/
465 http://onlinelibrary.wiley.com/doi/10.1002/ejsp.297/abstract

more people watch something go down, the less likely anyone is to take action. That's because when everyone else knows about something, it's easier to pass the buck and forget about it. If others aren't reacting we assume it isn't an emergency and won't intervene ourselves. One basic instinct is we ought to help others but another competing instinct is we ought to conform to the group. With so many of us aware of the injustices in our world but doing nothing about it, most of us fall into line and do the same.

Quote
Mark Twain – Author, Lecturer
"Whenever you find yourself on the side of the majority, it is time to pause and reflect"

Our reliance on existing experts and leaders

Most of us believe there are people smarter and brighter than us trying to figure out the world's problems so we don't give them too much thought. In reality there's almost nobody trying to figure out the world's problems. Our leaders are so busy trying to keep their own countries and businesses functioning that there's no chance for them to focus on the world's problems. Our competitive and individualistic culture means all our leaders are leaders of a small part of the world but we have no leaders for the whole world.

The responsibility lies with us all to understand the situation and demand it changes. Recognising systemic problems doesn't require rank or intelligence, just honesty of vision. Unfortunately, honesty of vision isn't easy for existing leaders because they're hamstrung by the prevailing dogmas of their existing institutions[466]. That's why fresh new ideas tend not to sprout from the minds of mainstream experts and existing leaders. Rather, most fresh new ideas sprout from the minds of regular people not heavily invested in existing institutions and existing ways of doing things.

The Monetary System is inherently self-perpetuating

The hierarchical nature of our system means those at the top tend to be those believing most in the existing way of life. To them the existing way seems pretty good. It's made them successful. As a result, they continue

---

466 http://www.guardiansofthestatusquo.com/

to promote the positivity they see in it.

Almost everything we see or hear on TV, in the news, in movies, on the radio, and in magazines, is all coming from the perspective of those prospering most from the existing situation. These aren't evil people, they're just people like the rest of us with views on the world that reflect their own experiences. It becomes a great defence mechanism of the system and part of the reason we never see the merits of money debated anywhere.

Very few of the poorest people support the Monetary System. They don't think it's fair, just, or efficient. But we don't hear from the poorest people, precisely because they're the poorest people. In contrast, very few of the richest people doubt the Monetary System. They don't think it's unrewarding, damaging, or ineffective. And these are the people we do hear from, precisely because they're the richest people.

We see from history that people at the top of any society will do everything possible to preserve the existing situation in which they're prospering[467]. This is not a conspiracy, it's a fact of human nature within a hierarchical society based on self-interest.

We don't recognise how bad things are

We only know the world we know. It's difficult for us to objectively assess our world.

Thought experiment
Imagine you're born into a future over-populated society. At birth you're randomly matched with another baby who was born on the same day. Once you both turn 18 you'll have to fight to the death – it's a standard population control measure. It's generally accepted as the way it is.

What would you do if you were born into a world like this? Would you spend the first 17 years of your life trying to change the system and create a world where this wasn't necessary? Or would you spend the first 17 years training to fight so when you turn 18 you give yourself every chance of winning and surviving?

This may seem like an extreme situation but when we look a little closer it isn't too dissimilar to life today. Today we're born into a society where

---

467 http://www.gutenberg.org/files/1232/1232-h/1232-h.htm

50% of the population live on less than $3 a day, so while they're technically alive, they aren't really living. How many of us spend the first 17 years of our lives trying to change this? And how many of us spend the first 17 years of our lives studying and training to get a good job so we can survive comfortably into adulthood?

The majority of us don't try to change the way it is. We do our best to survive within the system we're born into, regardless of how inhumane that system may be. There is nothing in neuroscience to suggest it would be any different if we were born into a society like the one described in the thought experiment above.

The change is too big for us to comprehend

For several thousand years, our civilisation has been based around hierarchy, money, ownership, governance, taxation, power, status, and competition. A Resource Based System wouldn't be based on any of these things. It would be a paradigm shift to everything our lives have been grounded in for thousands of years.

With the longevity of money, a radical change is easy to dismiss because of how different it is. Dismissing something purely on the grounds of it being a radical change is a logical fallacy though.

Quote
Bertrand Russell – Nobel Prize Winning Philosopher, Mathematician
"The fact that an opinion has been widely held is no evidence whatsoever that it is not utterly absurd"

We're largely powerless to choose our future

Today we feel like we have choices. Rather than genuine choice we have an illusion of choice. We have a dazzling array of choice in things that don't really matter but no choice in the important stuff. We have thousands of:

- Flavours of ice-creams
- Sizes and shapes of TVs
- Styles of clothing
- Mobiles phones
- Restaurants
- Flavoured drinks and candies

But we only have a handful of choices in the stuff that actually matters:

- Big Banks - controlling the cost and supply of money
- Big Oil companies - controlling the cost of almost everything we buy
- Major political parties - all doing pretty much the same thing and proposing no real change
- News organisations - distracting us with entertaining stories that mask the real issues
- Big Telco's – controlling the ease and cost at which we can communicate with others

This results in choices being consolidated to an elite few powerful leaders. They control our social direction, how much things cost, what we see, what we hear, and what we read.

Analogy

Think of our lives as a car heading down the highway. Today the car is being driven for us. Most of us don't know how we got in the car, we don't know the destination, we don't know the features of the car, we don't know the safety parameters of the car, as we pass people in other cars we don't know where they're going or what their motivations are. All we control is the song that plays as we go along... And even that is from a pre-defined list of acceptable songs.

Most people don't get the kind of car they want, or live in the house they want, or do the kind of job they want, or even have the lives they want. We live in the house we can afford, drive the car we can afford, and do the job that pays the bills. So do we really have choice?

Our energies are directed to the wrong challenges

Some people believe the biggest challenge we face is climate change, others say corruption, others say religion, others say poverty, others say education, and others say terrorism. We don't need to wade into the debate on which of these represents a bigger challenge because none of these are isolated challenges. They're all fragmentary by-products of our cultural mother-ship – the Monetary System. If we remove the Monetary System we also remove things like greed, waste, inequality, materialism, and so on. If we remove the Monetary System we'd overcome the things most people believe are the major challenges facing us today.

Unfortunately, very few of us are directing our energy and focus to the root of our problems (money). Instead most of us direct our focus passionately toward the symptoms (climate change, poverty, terrorism, etc) of the base problem (money).

10.6. What drives large-scale social change?

Quote
Thomas Edison – Inventor
"Discontent is the first necessity of progress"

History teaches us that large-scale social change results from a build-up of pressures within society. It isn't deliberately and independently instituted by existing leaders[468]. Rather, change happens when:

1. Things get bad enough for a large enough group of people, leading to a mass loss of confidence in the existing social structure[469].
2. The loss of confidence is complemented with a hopefulness that change can be successful[470].

When these conditions are met, revolution occurs and change happens[471]. Revolution doesn't have to mean violence and death, revolution can arise from changing our way of thinking.

With every day that passes, conditions become more amenable to revolution. People are becoming more aware of the immorality of money and the possibilities for positive social change in a world without money. But where are we at on this journey of shifting awareness?

10.7. A value and consciousness shift is well underway

Research
A public opinion poll by CNN in 2004 found that 89% of Americans believe there was a U.S government cover-up surrounding the planes that

---

468 http://www.beyondintractability.org/essay/social-structural-changes
469 http://www.lulu.com/shop/c-martins-r/utopia-or-deathhttp://www.lulu.com/shop/c-martins-r/utopia-or-death/ebook/product-20006465.html
470http://www.jstor.org/discover/10.2307/2770336?sid=21104924170561&uid=4&uid=3737720&uid=3739448&uid=2
471 Burton, John. *Conflict: Resolution and Provention.* (New York: St. Martin's Press, 1990), 247

crashed into the twin towers on September 11. Further, a poll by AM640 news found 85% of Canadians believe it was an inside job. Further still, a world public opinion poll in 2007 found almost 2 in 3 people believe Al Qaeda was not responsible for the 9-11 attacks.

The majority of people in the world believe that our leaders were – to some extent – involved in a plot to fly planes into buildings to kill their own people. Whether this actually happened or not is beside the point. The point is it represents a growing loss of confidence in the existing social structure.

9-11 is one prominent example but there's now many situations where those believing the conspiracy far outnumber those believing the official story[472,473,474,475,476]. Conspiracies are becoming mainstream while official stories are becoming fringe. This is an indication that people are losing confidence in the existing social structure. As people lose trust in the information provided by their leaders, conditions become increasingly acquiescent to social change.

Research
A longitudinal survey of public opinions of the news was carried out between 1985 and 2011. The survey highlights strong trends of public distrust in the way our news is run and the things we're being told: 66% of people now believe stories are often inaccurate – up from just 34% in 1985. 77% believe stories now tend to favour one side – up from 53% in 1985. 80% believe stories are often influenced by powerful people and organisations – up from 53% in 1985.[477]

Research
Research conducted across five continents shows that Generation Y (born 1985-2000) are now more interested in being fulfilled, doing something that matters, and doing social good, than they are with making money. This is in stark contrast to their parents – the Baby Boomers (born 1945-1965) – who've traditionally been more focused on earnings and status.

472 http://www.ncbi.nlm.nih.gov/pubmed/23847577
473 http://www.ncbi.nlm.nih.gov/pmc/articles/PMC2929157/
474http://www.jstor.org/discover/10.2307/3791630?sid=21104996075161&uid=4&uid=3737720&uid=3739448&uid=2
475 http://www.tandfonline.com/doi/abs/10.1207/s15324834basp1703_7#.VKl4wSvF-So
476 http://www.mirror.co.uk/news/world-news/ebola-conspiracy-theories-spreading-fast-3929922
477 http://www.people-press.org/files/legacy-pdf/9-22-2011%20Media%20Attitudes%20Release.pdf

This research illustrates a shift in values and consciousness, a realisation from younger generations that the story of money providing happiness is not quite holding up.[478]

This generational shift in values is now quantified across a wide range of studies[479,480,481,482,483]. These studies show the old power-driven, ego-centric model of life and success is crumbling and being smothered by emerging values such as compassion, empathy, and humanitarianism. The warmth and altruism within human nature is beginning to shine through.

Research
A survey across 107 countries shows more than half of us think our government is largely or entirely run by groups acting in their own interests rather than for the benefit of the citizens. Furthermore, people state they're ready to change this status-quo - almost 9 in 10 surveyed say they would act against corruption.[484]

These are inspiring results once again. They demonstrate for a fact that:

- The majority of people know the way the world works sucks
- The majority of people would change it given the opportunity

All that's needed now is a hopefulness that change can be successful. People need to know that viable alternatives exist. If people believe change can be successful they'll begin to speak out more freely and this new set of values will become more mainstream.

10.8. Can we change?

We have a great record of making long lasting social, behavioural, value, and belief changes that almost everyone thought was impossible. Social change has been a constant throughout history. Those changes have been from things like division, inequality, and segregation to things like unity,

478 http://www.iopenerinstitute.com/media/73185/iopener_institute_gen_y_report.pdf
479 https://hbr.org/2013/07/connect-then-lead/ar/1
480https://static1.squarespace.com/static/51ed234ae4b0867e2385d879/t/51fab9d9e4b0cc5aa44f3d20/1409519708244/evolution-of-fairness-in-the-one-shot-anonymous-ultimatum-game++.pdf
481 https://www.ketchum.com/sites/default/files/klcm_executive_overview_2014.pdf
482 http://onlinelibrary.wiley.com/doi/10.1111/j.1540-5885.2009.00344.x/abstract
483 http://www.scribd.com/doc/215704903/FP-Koenig-Eagly-2011
484 http://www.wingia.com/web/files/news/61/file/61.pdf

equality, and community.

Legal slavery has been abolished, coloured people are slowly gaining more equal rights (think Barack Obama, first coloured U.S President), women are slowly gaining more equal rights (many countries have had their first female leaders and women almost everywhere can now vote), gay people are slowly gaining more equal rights (gay marriage is now decriminalised in many countries), and animals are slowly gaining more equal rights (many countries have re-classified animals as beings and banned or severely limited their use in research).[485]

Looking back it seems obvious something like slavery is wrong. We struggle to understand how everyone just went along with it for so long. On the same note, in the future we'll probably look back with similar bewilderment at our inability to grasp the obvious fact of how wrong money is - with its inherent poverty, limitation, deprivation, and inequality.

Quote
Elizabeth Cady Stanton – Abolitionist, Suffragist
"The history of the past is but one upward struggle to equality"

Change is inevitable in the long run, providing we don't self-destruct first. It's not a question of if we change, it's a question of when and how. Will it be a violent and bloody breakdown in social structure that provides the trigger to motivate us to change? Or will we be more proactive? That's up to each and every one of us. It's our collective action that will determine our future.

The things that go viral online show we're addicted to positive content. Positivity is the main variable a piece of internet content should contain in order to successfully go viral. Positivity is the enduring thread that binds us together[486,487,488,489]. This is great cause for hope. It demonstrates that in spite of all the negativity built into our world today, there's a persistent

---

485 http://en.wikipedia.org/wiki/Animal_rights_movement
486 http://www.fastcodesign.com/3024276/evidence/these-scientists-studied-why-internet-stories-go-viral-you-wont-believe-what-they-f
487 http://jonahberger.com/books/contagious/
488 http://www.theguardian.com/media/2014/mar/16/how-to-make-something-go-viral-tips-buzzfeed
489 http://www.forbes.com/sites/kiriblakeley/2011/09/06/why-does-something-go-viral/

positivity within us. We want to be a part of something good, something great even, and we want to do it together.

10.9. We are not civilised yet

Quote
Konrad Lorenz - Zoologist
"I have found the missing link between ape and civilised man... it is we"

Kids in the future might learn about the time our society was run by those with the most imaginary paper – when everyone was trying to get as much as they could for themselves. This may be looked back on as the uncivilised period - until we became one species and acted in the interests of human kind. They'll probably look back on it as a brutal time in history, much like we look back on the Barbarian times today.

Kids in the future might wonder how we endured it for so long, especially with so much collective intellect and technology. We had all the tools for success but continued to operate in some sort of blind addictive worship to these pieces of imaginary paper.

Quote
Charles Eisenstein – Author, Public Speaker
"Most of us - even from a young age - have a sense of the wrongness of society. A sense that it's not supposed to be this way - that you're not supposed to actually hate Monday or be happy when you don't have to go to school. School should be something that you love, life should be something that you love"

Kids in a future moneyless society would've been immersed in an environment of co-operation, abundance, efficiency, collectivism, and altruism. They wouldn't have experienced any of the scarcity, limitation, deprivation, competition, ownership, greed, and corruption of the monetary era. Our grandkids could well be living in a civilised world like this but on the other hand – if we remain in the Monetary System - our grandkids could well be the last generation of hominids to enjoy a habitable Earth. Both are very plausible futures right now. Which future transpires will depend on the actions we take today.

10.10. Where to from here?

Quote

Oliver Wendell Holmes Jr – Supreme Court Jurist

"Man's mind, once stretched by a new idea, never returns to its original dimensions"

The next phase in our cultural evolution is to realise that simply looking out for ourselves and trying to earn money for ourselves is not the best we can do. We can be so much more if we design a social system that supports us in working together to create a society that's better for all of us collectively. In fact, if we want to survive in the long run we need to arrive at this realisation pretty quickly.

Shifting to a moneyless society isn't something we should blindly rush into though. It'll require extensive planning, examination, investigation, research, and a much deeper assessment of feasibility than we've conducted here in this book. Bringing this to life will require significant public support but before the public can make their voices heard the public needs to be aware of the possibilities.

As we've just seen, for change to be successful there are two pre-requisites:

1. A loss of confidence in the existing social structure
2. A hopefulness that change can be successful

We already have considerable evidence of a global loss of confidence in the existing social structure. What we don't appear to have is a hopefulness that change can be successful. This is the next step in the journey - widespread awareness that change can be successful. The abundant possibilities of a world without money need coverage in as many domains of public discourse as possible. Only then can we consider avenues to influence governments and institutions to take action.

So how do we raise awareness there's a viable alternative? Everyone who's read this book has made themselves aware, so the simplest way is to share this with others. That isn't really enough though. One book isn't going to transmogrify global consciousness and build a hopefulness that change can be successful. This type of information-heavy book does not appeal to everyone. That's part of the beauty of human diversity, we all resonate with different stuff. So we need people to produce their own content, their own way of telling the story of money and the alternatives for our future.

We can each put our own identity to it, whether it be in music, poetry, theatre, conversation, demonstration, podcasts, presentations, or videos. We all have our own unique talents, our own way of individually communicating with the world and sharing ideas. We just have to be careful to do it in a way that allows people to feel included and enlightened rather than frightened or offended.

Quote
Isaac Newton – Physicist, Mathematician, Philosopher
"Tact is the art of making a point without making an enemy"

The more content we can produce, the greater chance we have to provide hope that change can be successful. This is why we need more storytellers – people with an ability to communicate and share wisdom with others.

Quote
Maria Popova – Writer
"Wisdom is the application of information worth remembering and knowledge that matters, to understanding not only how the world works, but also how it should work. That requires a moral framework of what should and shouldn't matter as well as an ideal of the world at its highest potentiality. This is why the storyteller is all the more urgently valued today. A great storyteller - whether a journalist, editor, filmmaker, or curator – helps people figure out not only what matters in the world but also why it matters. Through symbol, metaphor, and association the storyteller helps us interpret information, integrate it with our existing knowledge, and transmute that into wisdom"

Anyone who doesn't see themselves as a storyteller can also get involved with a number of transitional communities, groups, and movements trying to bring a moneyless society to life (see references)[490,491,492,493,494,495,496,497,498,499,500,501,502,503,504]. Doing any of these things constitutes a positive effort to leave the world in a better place than we found it. Nobody can ask more than that.

While the evidence suggests we'll struggle to avert a catastrophic collapse of our global civilisation, we all have an ethical obligation to try. It's clear the human spirit is powerful and can overcome adversity against all odds. So where will we go from here?

Nobody knows. It would be naïve to attempt to predict it. We see from history the most innocuous things often provide the spark that leads to stirring global revolutions. Nobody knows what the future holds but we're all a part of it together and every action we take will contribute to it.

Quote
Margaret Mead – Cultural Anthropologist
"Never doubt that a few thoughtful committed citizens can change the world, indeed, it is the only thing that ever has"

Our actions today will define history tomorrow. What will history read?

490 http://www.moneylesssociety.com/
491 https://www.facebook.com/groups/224148967647327/
492 http://www.thezeitgeistmovement.com/
493 https://www.thevenusproject.com/en/
494 http://valhallamovement.com/
495 http://www.tromsite.com/
496 http://www.moneylessworld.org/
497 http://www.irbe.org/
498 http://www.theemergenceproject.org/
499 http://futurewewant.org/
500 http://a-r-k.us/us/welcome/
501 http://www.ic.org/
502 http://communityplanet.org/
503 http://moneyfreeparty.org.uk/viewpage.php?page_id=7
504 http://sustainablehuman.com/

ACKNOWLEDGMENTS

I'd like to thank everyone who contributed their own time free of charge to review the book and provide feedback. From Grace Nicholas and Denise Greer who reviewed very early drafts of the manuscript, through to Daniel Herbert, Wayne Greer, Tanya Basi, and Nick Shea who provided feedback on more advanced drafts. Your comments provided insights I would never have reached myself.

I'd also like to thank Tim Kavermann from Fuel Media for his help with digital design elements.

As a final note, I'd like to add that not all of those people mentioned necessarily support or endorse the ideas in this book. This is part of the reason their insights were so invaluable in making the book better.

87422521R00091

Made in the USA
Middletown, DE
04 September 2018